Won★der★lust

Won*der*lust

- verb
a journey into discovering the
    Wonder in your Woman

Rosie Ortiz

Copyright 2025 by Rosie Ortiz

All rights reserved.

No portion of this book may be reproduced, stored in a retrieval system, or transmitted in any form or by any means - electronic, mechanical, photocopy, recording, scanning, or other – except for brief quotations in critical reviews or articles, without the prior written permission of the publisher.

Printed in the United States of America

Book Cover Design by Nestor Ortiz

ISBN

First Edition

Creative Wonder House Publishing

To the one who yearns for a deeper connection within themselves and fulfillment that is long lasting. This book is for you. May you find the extraordinary in the ordinary and may you forever be **Wonderstruck**.

Men go abroad to wonder at the heights of mountains, at the huge waves of the sea, at the long courses of the rivers, at the vast compass of the ocean, at the circular motions of the stars, and they pass by themselves without wondering.
- St. Augustine

Contents

Preface

Introduction: Road Trips,
Wonder Woman, and the Family Manager　　*xi*

Chapter 1
Some-Kind-of-Wonderful　　**1**
Spiritual Health
Self-Discovery Questions　　*12*

Chapter 2
Wonder Women not Wander Women　　**13**
Mental & Emotional Health
Self-Discovery Questions　　*25*

Chapter 3
Wonder Factor　　**27**
Purpose
Self-Discovery Questions　　*41*

Chapter 4
Wonderful-NES　　**43**
Love & Romantic Relationships
Self-Discovery Questions　　*57*

Chapter 5
Wonder Works　　**59**
Career, Profession, or Job
Self-Discovery Questions　　*74*

Chapter 6
Wonder-Full 77
Financial Health
Self-Discovery Questions 92

Chapter 7
Wonder Land 93
Friendships & Community
Self-Discovery Questions 107

Chapter 8
Wonderstruck 111
Self-Discovery Questions 118

Conclusion – Wonder Seeker 121

Acknowledgments 125

Notes 129

Index 133

*My Favorite Things
& Recommended Reading* 135

Wonderlust Tips 137

About the Author 143

Bookings 145

Visit for Free Bonuses 146

Preface

Wonderlust is a journey of self-discovery and the search for inner fulfillment whose only access point is through honest self-reflection. It's a journey available to all, but one that few are willing to embark on because the depths of what we might find can be scary to face and can challenge those things we are comfortable with. It's a pilgrimage so personal that it will escort you into limitlessly exploring the deep places within and prompt you to rebuild yourself from the inside out.

Introduction

★★★

*Road trips, Wonder Woman,
and the Family Manager*

Road Trips

I wonder where we'll go next? That's always the question I have once we've come back from a trip. No sooner have we arrived and put the dirty laundry from our adventures in the wash when my mind begins to wander about the possibilities for our next journey. It's as if Dr. Seuss' words echo over and over in my mind, "Oh the places you'll go". I once read the best way to get through the everyday routine that can become somewhat of a rut is to always have a trip booked. Whether a one-night getaway, a long weekend, or an extravagant trip overseas, the excitement of knowing I'll be packing my bags soon and getting away is all I need to keep pushing through the everyday monotony.

Being from Florida, the first trip I have recollection of was Circus World. I grew up in Miami and with Orlando being just a short three-and-a-half-hour drive, that meant that long weekends could be spent in the most magical place on earth that others traveled across the world to visit. Though Circus World was not part of the Disney Parks, it was still in the general vicinity and another park we were able to visit because of its proximity. My dad loved the circus and for that reason it was obvious that this was a must see for our family.

All of our road trips to Disney meant we would wake up at 3a.m. and start the exciting journey before the sun came up. This trip to Circus World was no different. Ham and cheese or tuna sandwiches wrapped in aluminum foil were always on the lunch menu. They were carefully stored in the cooler that was packed away tight in our maroon Chevy Pinto's trunk along with chips and soda. This was the standard menu for any road trip. Aside from bathroom breaks, our only stop was to have lunch out of the back of our car, as all our money was to be saved for the entrance fees to the parks, and our budget motel; so, car lunches it was!

This particular trip was an adventure of its own. Our car broke down about 2 hours in, but we didn't let that stop us. As soon as we got it fixed, we were back on the road and just a couple of hours behind schedule. Interestingly enough, I don't remember much about Circus World itself. It seems most of the excitement took place on the shoulder of the road off of I95; at least for us kids. A bit underwhelming, Circus World closed down permanently just a short time after our visit. I can't say we were surprised.

Without a doubt, my sister's and my love for traveling came from our father. He passed this hobby on to us in the most zealous fashion. Very much the penny-pincher in regular day to day life, the only departure he had from his parsimonious way of being was when traveling. Fine dining during trips and nice excursions were the only times we ever saw him splurge. This was also when he was at his happiest.

This love for adventure is one that has followed me my whole life. Inspired by the Disney road trips that later turned into exploratory trips in the US and even some abroad, I was certain I was making the right decision when I dropped out of college to become a flight attendant. About six months after beginning my college career and failing all the classes I was enrolled in, I decided to set school aside and pursue my teenage dream of flying the friendly skies. Being uncertain of what exactly I wanted to do with my life at the time, this seemed like the perfect option. I could travel and get paid to do it. It made absolute sense.

For three years I got to travel the world and visited some of the most breathtaking places on earth that left me Wonderstruck. The picturesque sceneries I witnessed still live in my mind. Along my journeys, I made new friends, tried exquisite food, and learned about different cultures; all things I still think about today. Without a doubt, I reveled in the moment!

Eventually, that phase of my life came to an end, and I moved on to finishing my degree, and starting a family. Yet, despite the complete departure - no pun intended - from waking up in a different city every morning to being a full-time mom, wife, and teacher, this passion for exploration was something I would never get rid of. My father's handed down love of wanderlust revolutionized my life in more ways than one.

From the Amazon River to the Egyptian pyramids, traveling around the world was responsible for awakening an insatiable sense of Wonder-seeking in me. In time, it translated over into lusting after the most mesmerizing wonder I had ever come across: my inner wonder. Without a doubt, it was and continues to be one of the most awe-inspiring journeys I have ever been on where I continue to discover layers of myself that have existed all along. Out of this journey was born Wonderlust.

Introduction

Wonder Woman

Thinking back on my first experience with Wonder makes me realize just how much my definition of it has evolved, and my experience of what Wonder is has changed. I was introduced to Wonder Woman -- the action figure -- somewhere during my elementary school age. Just like so many other children I was in complete admiration of her strength, resilience, and power. She was everything I wanted to be as a little girl, and she represented a limitless version of what could be accomplished as a woman.

Enthralled by her looks, her invisible jet, her boots, and all the other astonishing parts that comprised this larger-than-life heroine, it never occurred to me that what made Wonder Woman so Wonder-full was deeply embedded in her and went so much deeper than what the eye could see. It wasn't until much later in life that I would discover this.

My definition of Wonder -- very child-like at the time -- was superficial at best. I've now come to realize that most people's concept of Wonder never outgrows this stage. Relegated to the same category as whimsical, magical, and happily ever after, most people's understanding of Wonder keeps it playful in nature and something to be found in fairy tales.

Though a light side to Wonder definitely exists, a deeply profound version does as well.

I've come to believe that Wonder is an actual gift from God. Having created us with everything we would ever need to be successful in this lifetime, our designer gave each of us individual purpose and along with that, He also gave us a sense of Wonder in connection to that purpose. This can be interpreted as the essence of what makes up our particular gift and in turn allows us to carry out our purpose.

The Family Manager

Our oldest daughter, Sky, or the family manager as she likes to be called, has always been of strong character. Her ability to question or push back on any given topic is nothing short of amazing. Conversations with her can be both frustrating and enlightening all at the same time. Her gift of getting others to not only see her point, but to buy into it, is what will one day make her a great attorney. Throughout the years and thanks to the great professors she's studied under, she has learned to fine tune this unique ability, and she has become a wonderful advocate for those groups she supports.

The essence of her gifting, or what I like to call her Wonder Factor, is her unwavering and passionate stance on any given subject coupled with

Introduction

her ability to persuade. Her individual purpose is to be a lawyer. After making this connection for herself, Sky decided she would be starting law school to pursue what she believes is her life's calling.

Not surprising, Wonder is one of the first things we lose when life gets difficult as it can be overshadowed by circumstances. It wasn't until I lost my personal Wonder that I realized it was possible to misplace it. Yet, the even bigger discovery, when I found that it could also be reinstated. I'll share more about that in the coming chapters.

It's important to keep in mind that this book is meant to be a tool to get you on the path of your own exploratory journey but it's not a means to a final destination. The journey into the discovery of oneself is one of constant evolution. As long as we are alive and breathing, we will have ever-changing feelings and experiences which in turn will lead us into new paths all in search of personal inner fulfillment. Wonderlust is simply a blueprint of seven different areas in our lives we can use to measure our success and conformities along the way.

My hope is that as you read through the pages of this book and explore the seven areas of Wonder outlined herein, that you will become immersed in your own journey of Wonderlust!

Before we continue, I'd like to tell you about the Wonderlust Affirmations you will find on the next page. I wrote this for me and for you specifically on those days when life gets hard and we can forget who we are. Flag the page it's on and make sure to read them any time you need a subtle reminder of your Wonder.

Introduction

Wonderlust Affirmations:

My Wonder factor is an internal one.

The thing that makes me so spectacular is so deeply engrained that even if I'm stripped of all the frills, I am still WONDER-full.

I am worthy of astonishment, worthy of admiration, and worthy to marvel over today just as I am.

CHAPTER ONE

★★★

Some-Kind-of-Wonderful
-Spiritual Health-

"All things proclaim the existence of God".
-Napolean Bonaparte

Whenever I hear the term Jack of all trades, I can't help but to immediately think of myself. Well, I suppose Jill of all trades would be more appropriate. Throughout the course of my life, I've held a variety of roles and positions which have allowed me to develop skills I didn't know I possessed, as well as provided room for me to explore different fields. My reach has been large and wide to the point where I have occasionally forgotten I held a certain function or role at some point in time.

Along my journey I've delved in careers such as flight attendant, dental assistant, realtor, phlebotomist, elementary school teacher, jewelry designer and maker, storyteller, and online English professor just to name a few. With my last role, prior to stepping into full-time entrepreneurship, being in Professional Development at a local non-profit. Every role I have ever held has taught me something different about myself and allowed me to develop new transferable skills that I continue to use till this day. Though not all of these roles came natural to me at the beginning, it was the effort and consistency I put in that allowed me to get better with each passing day and helped develop talents in me that I didn't know I possessed.

Learning Styles & Multiple Intelligences

In my last nine-to-five role in professional development, one of my tasks was training new instructors who would be working with the youth that we served on all aspects of the classroom. As part of this curriculum, one of the modules we would cover during onboarding of new hires was Multiple Intelligences developed by Howard Gardner. This was one of my favorite topics to cover. With so many personalities I came across during training, it was always impressive to see the concepts of this theory in practice in my personal classroom. Specifically, how we all learn in different ways and how we are all intelligent in different ways.

Of course, I couldn't teach this class without taking the assessment myself. This allowed me to better understand the theory and to have my personal outcomes as a reference. I must admit the first time I took the test I was surprised at some of the results. While some of my high scores were self-predicted and quite obvious, others came as a complete surprise and allowed me to understand myself better and the way I process.

- Side note-, if you haven't taken a multiple intelligence test, I highly recommend you do as it allows you to learn many different things about yourself including why you learn the way you do. I'm including a link to the assessment in the "My Favorite Things" page at the end of this book.

According to the scores from my personal assessment, my highest-ranking multiple intelligence was existentialism. This one was obvious and expected. However, the one that took me by surprise was Musical-Rhythmic Intelligence. I was sure this would be one of my lowest scoring areas. Having always thought of myself as having no musical abilities or inclination, it certainly caught me off guard to learn that there's a certain level of musicality in the way my mind processes information.

After studying this type of intelligence more deeply, I discovered that what makes someone have a high intelligence in a particular category isn't just the obvious. Many different layers exist to any given intelligence which means the way a particular intelligence presents itself in one person can vary from the next.

Wonderlust tip #1

Take a multiple intelligence quiz to learn more about the ways you are smart. I am including additional information about the quiz in *the My Favorite Things* section in the back of the book.

The Spiritual Lens

As mentioned before, prior to even taking the assessment, I knew I was an existentialist. From my perspective this meant that the validity of this whole theory hinged on whether or not this Multiple Intelligences assessment would be able to confirm that. For those that may not be familiar with the term, an existential type of multiple intelligence is one where a person has the ability to contemplate and grapple with deep philosophical questions about human existence and constantly Wonders about things such as the meaning of life and death and our place as it relates to all of this. This describes me to a tee.

The lens through which existentialists view the world is a spiritual one. Perhaps you've heard the saying widely attributed to French philosopher and Jesuit priest, Pierre Teilhard de Chardin, "We are not human beings having a spiritual experience; we are spiritual beings having a human experience." I believe most existentialists would agree with the core message of this saying. As for me, this sums up my views completely.

I can't tell you exactly when I began to see life through this angle. As far back as I can remember I have always pondered the questions of where exactly we came from, who created us, and where we are going after this earthly experience is over. Even as a young child I innately understood that there was a separation of body and soul, and my constant question was WHO we could credit this phenomenon to.

The formative years of my life brought some understanding of organized religion as we were practicing Catholics, and my sister and I attended Catholic school. Yet, this wasn't enough to satisfy the level of curiosity I had and the questions I continued to ask myself. At the age of fourteen, my mother began attending a Christian church and after visiting with her several times it became clear the theological doctrine they followed was one that resonated with me, and the questions I had were finally being answered. This went far beyond a theological practice for me and was the first time I recall having an actual experience with God that felt real. I have been in a personal relationship with Christ ever since.

The Highest Level of Wonder

Since the first time I took the Multiple Intelligences assessment, I have retaken it about two more times. It is said that just because you score low in a certain area doesn't mean that it will stay that way forever. In fact, the theory suggests that if we intentionally work on strengthening our low scoring areas, we can retake the test after some time and find that our intelligence level in said area may have increased. I find this part of the theory fascinating and have hope to continue increasing my mathematical abilities which unsurprisingly has been my lowest scoring area.

Though -Some-Kind-of-Wonderful- may not be a part of your life and existentialism might be your lowest scoring intelligence level, it is something you can become attuned to if you desire. Just like any other level of intelligence, you can develop this area and come into experiencing and knowing the highest level of Wonder that exists.

Though my objective in this book isn't to convince you of religion, God, or any type of doctrine, I'd be remiss and untrue to my definition of Wonderlust if I didn't acknowledge my belief of Some-Kind-of-Wonderful as an integral part in our search for Wonder. It's my perspective that Wonder outside of Him doesn't really exist. Though we may come upon Wonderous experiences and moments, even when we are not acknowledging God as the creator of it, it is a much more holistic and fulfilling experience when we do.

Being in touch with Some-Kind-of-Wonderful gives us the ability to walk through everyday life and find meaning in the everyday things. It allows us an opportunity to make sense of those things that seem senseless and to see our circumstances from a higher perspective. When Some-Kind-of-Wonderful is a participatory presence in our life, He can act as a guiding light and comfort during our hardest times. I often wonder how others who don't hold any type of spiritual belief manage to make it through difficult moments as it's hard enough to overcome life's predicaments, even with faith as a support system.

Wonderlust Tip #2

If Some-Kind-of-Wonderful isn't a part of your everyday life, look for ways to develop this area.

God-incidences

Part of finding Some-Kind-of-Wonderful in our lives involves searching in everyday things and situations. Many times, we can overlook what's right in front of our face because it just seems too easy, and well, too obvious. Yet, the ironic thing about Some-Kind-of-Wonderful, contrary to what we are inclined to believe, is that He can be found everywhere. It's important to keep in mind that God wants to be found by us, and thus He will show up in the details hoping that we will be curious enough to question His involvement.

This search for Some-Kind-of-Wonderful, which can feel unilateral on our end, is two-sided. As much as we search for Him, He will allow Himself to be discovered. Therefore, it becomes our job in true hide-and-go-seek fashion to search everywhere until we find Him. With this in mind, one of the most obvious places we should look is in coincidences or rather **God-incidences**.

Coincidence is defined by Webster's Dictionary as a remarkable concurrence of events or circumstances without apparent casual connection. For years, I lived life subject to such meaning. Whenever things worked out too perfectly, when I ran into someone just as I had finished speaking about them, or when hearing a song, I had just been singing, for instance, I did what most of us do and chalked it up to chance. Never giving moments like this a second thought is what I was programmed to do for years. After all, what or who could be responsible for such marvelous coordination if not pure happenstance?

That is, until one day in my pondering, after carefully analyzing some of the smallest details in my life and realizing that even fortuity at its best couldn't synchronize events with such perfection, I changed my outlook. Some-Kind-of-Wonderful must have been at work for things to have worked out in my favor as many times as they had. I would no longer credit a fluke for something that was so thoughtfully masterminded. It became clear to me then, that those things I once thought were serendipitous in nature were really **God-incidences**.

God-incidence: Moments where God was literally orchestrating a circumstance or event

Nothing short of majestic, God can be found in all things big and small, including the subtle moments in our everyday life. He awaits to be discovered so that His role can become a more prevalent one. With this discovery comes the sobering realization that He has been present and divinely orchestrating circumstances and events all along. And the even bigger discovery is that our inability to recognize Him never canceled Him out or His desire to be involved in our lives. Truly, He is the initiator of all Wonder-full things.

Throughout this book we will continue exploring Wonder in all its facets and I will let you decide the extent to which Some-Kind-of-Wonderful is a part of your journey. Though my recommendation, if you want the full experience of finding Wonder in your life, is to begin here.

Some-Kind-of-Wonderful Self-Discovery

1. What is your Source?

   _____

   _____

2. What are the pillars of truth in your life that you operate under?

   _____

   _____

3. Who or what do you rely on or turn to when life gets hard?

   _____

   _____

4. Have you taken a multiple intelligence test and if so, what is your highest intelligence?

   _____

   _____

CHAPTER TWO

★★★

Wonder Women not Wander Women
-Mental & Emotional Health-

"Wonder is the beginning of Wisdom"
-Socrates

Difficult times often teach us hard lessons that we wouldn't learn otherwise, of course, assuming that we are open to learning them. I have certainly had my fair share of challenges and though the lessons learned haven't always been immediate, time and intentional inner work have helped me grow from those experiences. One of my collective takeaways from the hardships I have endured has been that if one part of our lives is in disarray and not dealt with, it's only a matter of time before the other parts of our lives are affected by those unresolved issues as unresolved issues are contagious.

As holistic beings we must recognize that each part of our lives contributes to our success as a whole. For this reason, when we face adversity it's important to deconstruct the experience and use it to gain a deeper understanding of ourselves and most importantly find healing, lest those hurts transfer over into other areas of our life eventually causing us to go into a state of wandering.

WANDER:

To ramble or rove without a fixed course or purpose

Wonderlust tip #3

Take the Wonderlust "Best Version of Yourself" inventory to check for your level of harmony in each area of life. This is available as a downloadable format and printable version in the free book bonuses when you visit wonderinyourwoman.com.

Mind Wandering

There is a statistic that says as humans we mind wander for about forty seven percent of our waking hours. For those that might not be familiar with the term, mind wandering simply means that there is no active thinking related to the task at hand. This can define moments like those when we are standing in line at the bank, typing on our computer, or even when we are driving. Though we are physically doing one thing, our minds are disconnected from the current moment and just going through the motions as we wander about other things: usually of little to no importance.

Though mind wandering is something we are all guilty of doing at some point, there exists a perpetual state of wandering that can be extremely detrimental. One that will keep us living outside ourselves, going through the motions of daily life but disconnected from our core thoughts and feelings. Often introduced to us by our subconscious mind after a period of unresolved issues in our life, wandering is an internal coping method that provides the mental and emotional disconnect needed for not having to challenge our dissatisfaction with our current lifestyle, mindset, or lack of purpose.

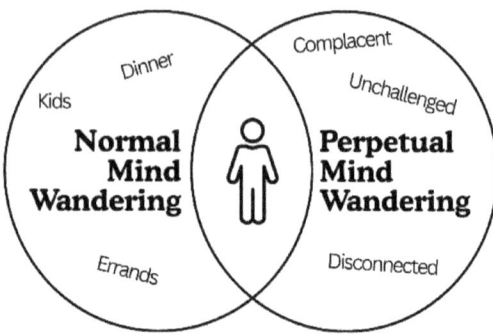

Wander Woman

At first glance, being what I call a wander woman might seem like a good approach for not having to deal with our feelings of inadequacy. It might even feel unburdening to live a life where you're only accountable for your reaction to your immediate situation or condition. With no one having any expectations of us (to include ourselves), what starts off as a care-free way of living soon turns into a lifestyle that is tolerant of all things.

I say this from a place of experience as I subscribed to being a wander woman for more years than I care to admit. Like most other women who adopt this passive lifestyle, it was a way to find a semblance of peace in what felt like mental and emotional exhaustion. For years, both personally and professionally, the best description of my life was to say it was aimless, without purpose, and with no specific plan, goals, or boundaries.

Leaving everything in my life to chance meant that I was open to whatever came my way - good or bad - and felt a sense of relief in not having to take responsibility for the happenings of my own life.

In short, *Life was happening TO me.*

As I mentioned before, unresolved issues are contagious, and this passive type of living was a result of several unresolved circumstances and on-going issues in my life that had begun to spill over into other areas. As much as we'd like to compartmentalize the different areas of our life, the integrated way in which we are created doesn't allow for separation of mindset, at least not long-term. If a mindset lingers long enough as it pertains to one specific area of our life, it eventually overtakes the whole operating system leading us into a completely wandering state. This is what the toxic marriage I was in did to me.

Being a wander woman allowed me to be complacent and not have to challenge those things that were familiar and offered a sense of security, in spite of being unhappy with them. A bad marriage and an unsatisfying career were both a part of this double-edged sword in my life. They offered familiarity and security that trumped any sort of questioning or self-reflection, which in turn allowed me to continue living an unchallenged and uninterrupted life. With my mindset rooted in the belief that - this was as good as things were going to get for me - (in all aspects) wandering, allowed me to accept my circumstances for what they were and gave me the peace I so desperately needed at the time.

Many times, interpreted as a free way of living without the pressure of responsibility or accountability to ourselves or others, wandering keeps us anything but at liberty. Yet, those who are drifting through life, much like I was, are fooled into thinking they are free. With no destination in mind as well as lack of goals or direction, wander women are easily accepting of where this unfocused path may lead them whether mentally, physically, or emotionally. Moreover, the truth about wandering is it's only an illusion of liberty and the freedom it offers is more-so based on limitations.

Just like mind wandering can put us in a state of idleness for moments at a time, chronic wandering can keep us living a stagnant and unproductive life. This way of living keeps the wanderer bouncing around seeking momentary satisfaction and never grounding themselves in anything that will give them long-term results or fulfillment. When we choose to be wander women, we are taking a path that will keep us victim to whatever circumstances we are experiencing at the moment and resolved to taking a submissive role in our own experiences and life. The good news is that being a wander woman is a choice and not an assigned task.

Wonderlust tip #4

Unresolved issues are contagious and the perfect incubator for creating *Wander Women*. Don't be the wrong type of superhero. We are *Wonder Women not Wander Women!*

Wonder in your Woman

I often get asked how I chose the name of my brand, *Wonder in your Woman*. As silly as it might seem, the name came to be after an office costume contest I participated in and won many years back. I'm sure you've guessed by now I dressed up as Wonder Woman. No surprise there. With a paid day off at stake, I was going to do everything in my power to win the contest. And I did. I left that day, elated that my effort in piecing this costume together didn't go unnoticed and most importantly one paid day off richer.

Yet, the biggest win that day had nothing to do with the costume and everything to do with the person I became when I was wearing it. To think it took a costume contest to draw out the wonder in my woman that had been lost for so long, makes me realize God really does work in mysterious ways!

For transparency's sake I must disclose that the costume alone did nothing magical. Yes, I felt confident, empowered, and in control of all things while wearing it, and I'd be withholding information if I didn't share, I felt important too.

--Everything I didn't feel when I wasn't wearing the costume--.

In fact, I felt all the things we believe a superhero to be. But in reality, it was the reflection that took place when I took the costume off that made the biggest impact.

Before I share the technicalities of my specific experience, I must let you in on the fact that interruption is the key component to finding our Wonder. Anytime there is a break in the continuity of a certain pattern, behavior, or feeling in our life, we can feel challenged to the point of wanting to push back in order to keep our peace of mind. But it's important to understand that finding our wonder begins with an interruption of everything we know to be familiar and secure. It's only through deep exploration and spotlighting of our deficiencies that we create room for growth and to become wonder women. This, of course, when followed up with making the necessary changes in our lives and doing the inner work. Wondering doesn't seek to accommodate us but to challenge us to come higher.

My case wasn't any different. When I allowed myself to sit in all the feelings of disruption that came with taking the costume off instead of turning away from them, I opened myself up to stepping into a higher level of wonder in my life and simultaneously a better version of myself. For the first time in a long time, I questioned my complacency with all the things that were wrong in my life as well as where my satisfaction lay. This interruption to everything I understood as factual at the time caused me to incessantly question why all the blissful Wonder Woman feelings couldn't be mine on a permanent basis and not borrowed only while I wore the costume.

This was my first experience of being **Wonderstruck** and the beginning of finding the Wonder in my Woman, although I will confess that the process is an ongoing one with many levels of self-discovery.

Contagious Confidence

As a child I often thought about - what made Wonder Woman so wonder-full?!?- and my answer always lied in the exterior factors; her invisible jet, the boots etc. It wasn't until after this costume contest that my perspective changed and for the first time I observed her as a woman instead of a superhero. It was then that I realized all the outside things were just frill and that in fact everything that made her who she was wasn't separate from her. Instead, I realized they were attributes that were so deeply engrained in her and it was the hard moments she went through that served as a spotlight for those virtues.

This brought me to the realization that the **Wonder Woman** feelings I so desired were always permanently mine and that the hard moments in my life didn't ever cancel them but were there to draw out everything that already existed. This was the moment of transference of belief for me and the first time I realized life didn't have to happen to me but rather for me. What started out as borrowed confidence from nothing more than a fictional character began to take deep root in me. Turns out confidence can be contagious too.

Though you may never experience a transformation of this nature whose catalyst is a superhero, there are many sheroes that walk among us daily. Women who we can catch confidence from and whose lives exemplify what it is to be a wonder woman; not settling and operating in their highest level of wonder. Women who have confronted their dissatisfaction instead of turning away from it and have accepted the challenge to rise higher, do more, be more and find true satisfaction in every area of their lives solely for themselves.

Wander to Wonder

Although, there is only a one letter difference from *Wander* to *Wonder* the outcome of being grounded in one or the other can mean the difference between living a subpar life or one of passion and purpose. Here are a couple of key differences between the two.

- ***Wander*** promotes familiarity and complacency. It reinforces that feeling safe and/ or secure in what's familiar is above feeling happy or satisfied. Poses as a safety net that promises security all the while keeping us bound.

Root Mindset: Life is happening ***TO*** me

- ***Wonder*** promotes disruption and exploration. It probes our current situation and causes us to question how satisfied we are with it.

Root Mindset: Life is happening *FOR* me

Wonderlust tip #5

Practice incorporating the Wonderlust mindsets which affirm the belief that life is happening for you not to you. These are available as a downloadable format and printable version in the free book bonuses when you visit wonderinyourwoman.com.

Wonder not Wander Self-Discovery

1. Wondering causes disruption. What could use disruption in your life?

   _____

   _____

2. What areas of your life have you previously found yourself Wandering in?

   _____

   _____

3. Is there an area that you are Wandering in now?

   _____

   _____

4. What are those things that you have settled in or for in your life?

   _____

   _____

5. How satisfied would you say you are in the following areas? Rate the areas below by using the following rating system.

> (1) not satisfied
> (2) barely satisfied
> (3) neutral
> (4) somewhat satisfied
> (5) completely satisfied

-Career _____

-Finances _____

-Marriage or Life Partner _____

-Health (Mental, Emotional, physical) _____

-Relationships (friends & Family) _____

-Spiritual Life _____

-Dreams / Personal Growth _____

CHAPTER THREE

★★★

Wonder Factor
-Purpose-

"There is no greater gift you can give or receive than to honor your calling. It's why you were born. And how you become most truly alive".
– Oprah Winfrey

Oftentimes, overshadowed by circumstances, our Wonder, is the key component to living a life of purpose. The famous Bahamian evangelist, Myles Munroe, once said, "The graveyard is the richest place on earth, because it is here that you will find all the hopes and dreams that were never fulfilled". If there's one thing I knew from an early age it was that I didn't want to leave this world without fulfilling my God given purpose. Since I can remember, I have always placed an enormous amount of value on using the gifts we are given.

In fact, there's nothing that brings me greater joy than seeing someone operate in their zone of Wonder. Whether it's a scientist explaining a method, a chef creating a delicacy, or an artist bringing something to life on canvas, watching someone do what they love brings me great joy and gives me a warm fuzzy feeling in my heart.

Search Deep

Not surprisingly, my zone of Wonder is helping others find theirs, specifically when it's been compromised or forgotten. As certain as I am of that now, -- that this is my life's purpose --, there was a time when I wasn't sure what my Wonder was. It can be somewhat frustrating when your Wonder isn't as obvious as the next person and you find yourself questioning if you even have one. Singers will obviously sing, and dancers will obviously dance, but what happens when your gift isn't as visible to the naked eye as everybody else's? Does it mean that upon creation, during the passing out of gifts you were overlooked? In short, no. Everybody has a Wonder Factor. But what it does mean is that you might have to search a little deeper than the next person to find it.

Recently, I spoke at an event whose underlying theme was finding success in midlife. This group of women, who were professionals and extremely successful in their life endeavors, attended in hopes of finding guidance and inspiration about what the second part of their life could look like. Many of them questioned whether they had more to give outside of what they had already accomplished. It was a pleasure to share my core message of *discovering the Wonder in your Woman* with them that day and getting them to see that Wonder isn't beholden to a timeline.

In other words, just because we may max out in our career in one season of life doesn't mean that we have exhausted all the Wonder ever afforded us. On the contrary, the magical thing about Wonder is that so long as we are breathing, there's more where that came from. Just maybe in a different form.

Wonderlust tip #6

As the essence of our gifting, Wonder can take on a different shape depending on the phase of life we are in. The outlet might not always look the same, but its core faculties are always there.

Bridge into Purpose

Soren Kierkegaard said, "Life can only be understood backwards, but it must be lived forwards". Understanding this truth is imperative to find our Wonder. In fact, it's key and the first step. When Wonder is elusive, our starting point to discover it should always be looking at our past. It's here that many times we find our Wonder hiding in plain sight. Though often it looks different than what we think.

I'm a proponent of the idea that pain can be a bridge into purpose if we allow it to be. Most people don't make the association between stumbling blocks in life and purpose yet, it is those same stumbling blocks that many times unveil the Wonder that has always existed within us and was waiting to be revealed. It's up to us to make the connection between pain and purpose and then allow our Wonder to be established as the bridge between the two.

Prior to discovering my Wonder, when I allowed life to happen *to me* and not *for me*, it would have been a difficult thing to imagine how any of my hurt at the time would ever make "sense". The disarray of my life as a whole, and in particular my messy marriage, was anything but purposeful in my eyes. Like others who wander, I was unable to see past any of my circumstances. That is until the day I decided to start taking ownership of my life and an active role in its outcome. This is what prompted me to first look back. Looking back has a way of making sense of a lot of things in life so long as we are keeping an eye out for the big picture.

It always amazes me to see my daughter Rain, put puzzles together. The more pieces to any given puzzle there are, the more she enjoys them. One thousand plus is her preference. She will usually throw all the pieces on our dining room table and spend several hours a day working on it until she manages to put the whole thing together. Patience is not a virtue I possess and so just watching her work on this, day after day, builds up a certain level of anxiety within me.

On the rare instance that I decide to help for a moment, all the different pieces that don't make sense or don't seem to fit where I think they should usually defeat me within minutes. It's not until she's completed the puzzle that in admiration, I can clearly see the Wonder of the whole picture and how each piece had a purpose. This is exactly how looking back at our life works. After thoughtful observation we can begin to see how one event in our past connects to another event and eventually, if we allow it, can lead us to purpose.

Connection, Retrospection, Admission

I first discovered this whole connection process during the costume contest days. The discrepancy in my confidence over who I was with the costume versus who I was without it prompted me to begin searching for what was obviously missing in my life. After all, this double personality thing wasn't a normal feeling to be experiencing. I didn't know it at the time but what I was looking for was my Wonder.

This journey to finding my wonder didn't happen overnight. It was a four-part process of:

- *retrospection*
- *connection*
- *admission* and
- *personal growth*.

It took many nights of candid conversation with myself to confront and acknowledge all the areas I was settling in and to try and pin them back to their root cause. I began with the failing marriage and worked my way down from there to include the unfulfilling career and every other area of my life I felt I was being complacent in.

This was my first face to face encounter with the dissatisfaction that was looming so heavily over my life at the time. No sooner had I allowed myself to acknowledge my disappointments, my failures, and most importantly, my part in allowing things to get as far as they did when I found myself making connections between my circumstances.

When we intentionally decide to stop Wandering, the puzzle pieces of our life can finally begin to make sense. In my specific case, little by little I began to see the big picture and how a long-term toxic marriage was affecting all the other areas of my life. Moreover, the loss of identity became clear. I didn't know who I was as a wife, as a professional, as a woman, and I walked around seeking satisfaction in momentary pleasures to fill this void.

All the details in our story are important and it is imperative that we acknowledge them for what they are and how they've impacted our situation. Doing this will allow us to better identify how all the different facts of our story play into the big picture which will subsequently help us build the bridge into purpose. More on that in a bit.

Theres a technique I've watched Rain do when she's putting the complicated puzzles together where she begins by grouping similar colors, pieces of images, and shapes. This "making sense" of the pieces makes it easier for her to begin connecting them all together when she's ready to start. She then compares the main picture on the box and what the outcome should be and starts to connect the pieces based on this.

It's very interesting to observe how all the individual pieces which served no purpose by themselves or even bunched up together on the table begin to take on meaning when they are connected and inserted into the right place. Before you know it as each piece is carefully adjoined to the rest, together, they begin to tell a story and lead you to realize that their presence was absolutely necessary for the whole picture to make sense.

The road to discovering our Wonder is one of many steps. It begins with being ***retrospective*** about how we've gotten to where we are, followed by making the ***connections*** between those deeply profound and life routing moments. Of course this is just the starting point. It's important to note that during this process of reflection things might begin to feel worse before they feel better. This is because in order to move forward freely it will feel like we are first taking a step back. Many may lose heart as the self-honesty required during this stage of finding our Wonder will bring up past grievances both involuntary or those we may have brought upon ourselves.

This initial stage of finding our wonder will require us to be fully committed to the process, knowing that experiencing ill feelings is part of the journey and indicating that we are right on track. As we work through these feelings it will bring us to the third step in our process; ***admission***. It's here where we have the opportunity to own every part of our story -- the good and the bad -- and once we do, we are ready to tackle the final part in our wonder discovery journey which is ***personal growth.***

This last part is just as important as the others in bridging the gap from pain into purpose as it places us in the position to recognize, develop, and refine skills that wouldn't have been able to emerge had it not been for our trials and challenges. In addition, it's in personal growth that we heal thoroughly from our experiences. This step is also what will ensure that the newfound wonder arising from within us can become the bridge into purpose. It's crucial that we don't skip this step otherwise, we will end up with abilities that are never put to use in the right space.

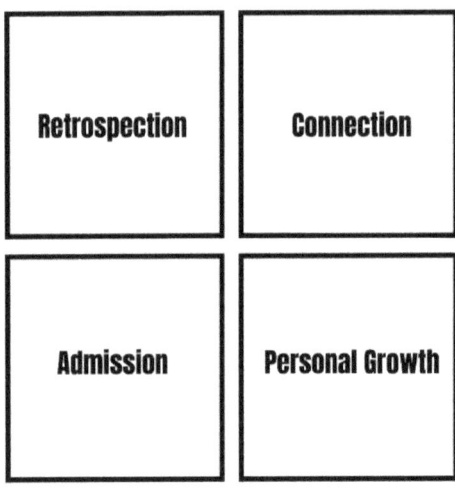

Wonderlust tip #7

Sometimes, the only way out is through. We can't avoid the feelings that come from connecting the pieces but its only through the connection that the disarray begins to make sense and takes on order.

Personal Growth & Imaginary Boots

Personal growth plays a pivotal role in our journey of discovering our Wonder. It is not enough to go through the process of retrospection, connection, and admission without committing to doing the internal work necessary to make sure we measure up to the calling of our Wonder. This is the step that prepares us to carry out our purpose; practically speaking.

During my journey of self-exploration and after going through the different stages, I quickly realized that without personal growth I would never be able to step into the next purposeful phase of my life. Working through our issues is key to putting the puzzle pieces of our life together but fully walking in our wonder will require more from us. Inevitably our challenges will cause us to develop strengths we didn't know we had but unless those are identified, cultivated, and trained, they won't be of much use for us or anyone else.

This initially dawned upon me when it hit me that walking around in my Wonder Woman boots, everywhere I went, wasn't going to be possible. I say that tongue-in-cheek of course, but my sense of security was directly tied to that costume -- the boots in particular -- and as mentioned before, I didn't know how else to fully own the feelings they inspired in me.

This is when I decided that nothing could stop me from wearing my imaginary boots. And so, I did. For some time anyway, until I finally completed the internal work required to properly heal and subsequently walk around without the boots, being solely secure in just being me.

Part of my personal growth plan meant processing through feelings, setting goals, embracing challenges that were out of my comfort zone, learning from my failures, mindset-shifting, and learning how to be assertive. These were some of the areas I worked on in the initial stage of personal growth. By default, my years' worth of personal challenges had also caused me to develop a certain level of resilience, grit, and emotional intelligence which could now be put into use. Eventually, after some real inner change had taken place, I was able to take the skills that the challenges had helped me develop in combination with this new secure version of myself to exercise my Wonder factor and walk in my purpose. Not only did the whole picture make sense now but I could finally see how my pain could be a bridge into purpose. You'll learn more about that in chapter five under Exercising My Wonder Factor.

And the best part…I did it without having to wear my imaginary boots.

Wonderlust tip #8

It's in personal growth that the wonder factor we may have been oblivious to becomes evident. This part is ongoing and crucial and cannot be skipped as it's what assures our character measures up to our calling.

Ongoing Development

As an avid reader with a very busy life, I have to be very intentional about scheduling time daily to read. I read not only for pleasure but for the knowledge I acquire from every book I get my hands on. My go-to genres are self-help, faith, biographies, positive psychology, and my most recent interest, business.

At the beginning of the year, I decided to be intentional about incorporating business books as this is an area I want to grow and expand my knowledge in and will also be of benefit in my entrepreneurial journey. Not my typical selection, the business genre has been a building blocks experience for me. Where I started with basic knowledge and information, I now have a broader understanding of certain concepts that I was previously very limited in. My business curiosity has grown beyond just books, and I now incorporate podcasts, YouTube videos and any other modes of instruction that I feel might add some value to my current understanding.

This is part of my current personal growth plan for this particular area of my life. One thing I have learnt throughout my life is that we must constantly grow and get better in the particular stage of life we find ourselves in. In an age where information is abundant, there is no excuse for not improving and learning from others who have already walked the path we find ourselves navigating.

Wonder Factor Self-Discovery

1. What is your Wonder factor?

   _____

   _____

2. Are you currently operating in your Zone of Wonder?

   _____

   _____

3. What connections can you make between those past events in your life and how have they impacted you or affected your life today?

   _____

   _____

4. What areas in your life could use personal growth?

   _____

   _____

5. What skills have your past challenges developed in you?

   _____

   _____

6. Are you using those skills in any area today? If so, where or in what capacity?

   _____

   _____

7. What is that thing you wish you could do?

   _____

   _____

CHAPTER FOUR

★★★

Wonderful-NES
-Love & Relationships-

"Love is patient, love is kind. It does not envy, it does not boast, it is not proud".
1 Corinthians 13:4

If there's one thing I'm grateful for it's second chances. Historically, it seems that in every area of life, I've always been that one person that gets things right the second time around. Whether my career, finances, marriage or any other area that would be considered a pillar, it usually takes me two good tries before I can reach a certain level of achievement that others reach in the first go around. This innate pattern in the way I function is one I noticed a few years back, but it has definitely been present since childhood. Where others always seem to be ahead of me and attaining a certain level of success, it always takes me a moment to catch up.

As frustrating as this can be, I've also observed that this delay in reaching certain accomplishments, that can many times feel like a flaw, can actually be a blessing. One that pays dividends at the end.

Second Chance Win

Some time back, I saw a friend post a video on social media of his son competing in an out of state track competition. It was quite impressive to see the gift this small statured young man had of taking the win just as the race seemed to be coming to a close. Throughout the duration of the race, he would linger in the back. Then, just as the race was coming to its final moments, he would break out of the pack and in an unforeseen way take the lead, ultimately winning the race in a truly show stopping fashion.

He had a skill level that was unique, and others' underestimation of him due to his size made for an even more exciting win. This was true for every race he participated in during that competition. Each time, it was a glorious win; unexpected, coming in from behind, and displaying mastery upon completion!

This is the perfect depiction of what second chance experiences have been for me in the past, and what I believe anyone's with the right amount of ambition and clarity about what they want to achieve can be.

> Lingering in the back
>
> Unexpected to win
>
> Breaking free from the pack
>
> Coming in from behind
>
> Taking the lead
>
> Mastery

WONDERLUST

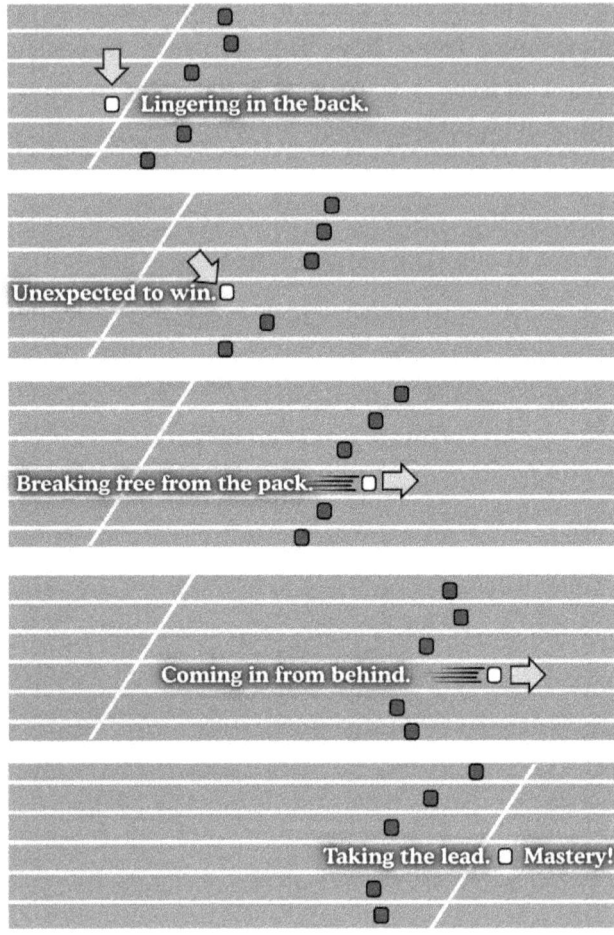

Wonderlust tip #9

The most glorious wins are often the unexpected ones. The delay might make you feel behind schedule but even 11:59 is before midnight.

Determination coupled with a second chance allows us to not only catch up and make up for lost time but surpass society's expectations of what second chance outcomes should look like as underestimated as we may have previously been. Through these experiences, I have come to learn that second chances are not only just as bonafide as first ones, but they can in fact be better. This concept applies to third chances, fourth chances, and all the chances beyond as well.

Of course, coming to this conclusion took some practice, with my best second chance outcome to date – that being my marriage to my husband, Nestor. Without a doubt he is what I call my **Wonderful-Nes**. And yes, it worked out pretty convenient that I could name this chapter after him. Just another time I feel God was casually winking at me while orchestrating this God-incidence. Although Nestor is the inspiration for this chapter and as much as I could go on about him specifically, my purpose isn't necessarily to tell you about him, but rather to highlight what life with the right person can be like.

Our spouse or partner in life plays a big role in our success or failure in all things. So, let's explore second chance relationships.

You Don't Know What You're Missing

There's nothing that can make us recognize the value of what we currently have more than going through a period in life when we don't have it. Whether a job, financial security, health etc., this sense of appreciation is heightened when we experience lack in said area. I suppose you could say lack builds appreciation. Yet, in an ironic way, many times, when we are living in deficiency of a particular thing or in a particular area, we are unable to identify what the best fix to meet our need is.

For example, suppose that you have never tasted strawberries. It would be safe to assume that despite having a craving for a dessert made from fruit, you would never consider strawberries as an option. Moreover, when strawberry season came around and you heard all the chatter about strawberry shortcakes or strawberry milkshakes you wouldn't feel as though you were missing anything because it was nothing you were familiar with. Yet perhaps if you tried them, after a lifetime of not having done so, you would then realize what you had been missing out on all those years. You might even like them so much that from then on you would make sure to get your fill of strawberry desserts whenever they were in season. -- Obviously, not everyone likes strawberry desserts, but you get the point. --

This same feeling of lack combined with the ignorance that something better exists, is responsible for countless unhappy and toxic relationships. You don't know what you're missing if you've never had it.

When it comes to relationships, length doesn't always equal success nor does it equal happiness. We can't deny that there are plenty of long-term relationships and marriages that have lived happily ever after, but the determining factor of that isn't measured by the time. My seventeen-year marriage for example, lasted as long as it did not because it was a good marriage but rather because I believed the popular myth of *"this is as good as it's going to get for me"*, like so many others do.

Just like the strawberry example, I had no clue that something better existed that could fulfill my needs or desire for more. I was oblivious to the fact that there was a better way to both love and be loved and that by accepting the whole *"this is as good as it's going to get"* theory, I was shortchanging myself of the grandest love I could ever experience; Wonderful-NES.

The Only Reason You Need

That is, until Some-Kind-of-Wonderful intervened in my life. At times, those moments that have the greatest impact on us are actually quite casual. And many times, they can even be as simple as everyday conversation. I still remember the phone call with an old friend I hadn't spoken to in years and holding my breath to learn of the reason she and her ex-husband had gotten a divorce.

I knew in my heart what she was about to share had to be monumental and would surely justify this decision. After all, this was one couple no one ever imagined would separate. What she said next was the simplest yet most profound thing I had ever heard. In fact, it was what gave me permission to want something more out of a marriage and to realize I wasn't selfish about wanting it.

"He didn't love me the way I needed to be loved".

That was it. That was the life changing moment. Though not as monumental and shocking as I had anticipated, hearing the exact thoughts I had felt for years spoken by someone else as a valid enough reason for her decision was life changing. It was enough to make me realize that *"this is as good as it's going to get for me"* wasn't a reason to stay in a relationship but an excuse.

Yet perhaps the biggest takeaway from our whole conversation was that just as my sweet friend, I also didn't need a reason to justify myself and my wanting more out of a marriage, to anyone. The only reason that counted was the one that made sense for me:

I hadn't been loved in the way I needed to be. And that was enough.

And I hadn't been wrong all those years in expecting more. That was all I needed to move forward.

Loving ourselves as women and putting ourselves first isn't just about getting out of the abusive relationship. Although, this is certainly a reason that warrants doing so. Many times, we are searching for that one reason that is big enough to call it quits when the whole time the only reason we need is that the relationship is not a satisfying one. This reason alone warrants putting ourselves first. Before anyone gets the wrong idea, I am not promoting divorce, and I certainly believe that you should work on your marriage or partnership. All relationships require work and will have their ups and downs. However, when a marriage is one that's depleting, toxic, dangerous, identity stripping, a poor example to the children involved, or narcissistic in nature, it may not be salvageable. It's in this instance that I recommend asking yourself "Am I being loved the way I need to be loved?"

Wonderlust tip #10

No one is going to give you a reward for how long you can stay in a relationship that you shouldn't be in (even if there are children involved). Choosing yourself and what's best for you isn't selfish, it's healthy.

Love and be Loved

Nestor and I often wonder whether soul mates exist. The question pops up every now and then as we acknowledge the connection he and I have is different than any other we have ever experienced. Soul mate or not, we both agree that life has been better for us after we met each other. I often refer to him as my *"retroactive love"*. In short, he is all the love that I didn't receive in years past, but was owed, all packed into one human being that is him.

You see, I believe that some kind of Wonderful created each of us with the right to give love and receive love, all in that unique and special way that each of us needs. With that need being as different as we are people, we deserve not only to receive the type of love we desire but we should learn to expect it as well. This is where many of us go wrong when we don't recognize our need to be loved in a certain way, as valid, and choose to accept less in return.

There is a very popular book on the subject titled *The 5 Love Languages* by Gary Chapman that explores five different ways of expressing and receiving love and the joy that comes from being in a relationship where these are honored. I recommend you read it to explore the subject further. The information is included in the *My Favorite Things* section found in the back of the book.

By nature, as women, we are caregivers and through the demands society places, to include raising a family, taking care of a home, running a business, working a full-time job, and the many other roles women may take on, we are taught to put ourselves last in the hierarchy of needs to be met. Although selfless in nature, this puts us in a compromising position. As such, expecting to be loved in any way besides what we are already receiving from a partner can make us feel as though we are asking for too much. Thus, leading us to settle for less than we deserve and less than what each one of us needs in order to feel fulfilled based on our individual love requirements.

Depending on the partner we have, the communication that exists, and the effort placed into correcting the deficiency, this can lead to a loss of identity and subsequently an unhappy and unhealthy relationship if not corrected. Loss of identity in a relationship is one of the fastest ways to lose our

Wonder. Wonder exists in authenticity and losing sight of who we truly are, our needs, our desires, and our expectations is a sure way to become stagnant in our emotions and consequently our endeavors.

--Remember, unresolved issues are contagious--

The right person by our side can catapult us into being the best version of ourselves and the wrong person can suppress us and strip us of the ability to know the difference. If we are blind to the source of a problem -- in this case recognizing the relationship as such -- it becomes much more difficult to mitigate and instead, we find ourselves in a perpetual state of tolerance and dissatisfaction.

An important thing to keep in mind is that it's never too late to choose ourselves and to put our emotional and mental well-being first. It is in taking this first step towards self-love that we make room for someone to come into our lives and love us in the way we need and for who we actually are. This is the most liberating type of love as it allows us to be our truest self in every sense of the word and to be unapologetically secure in who we are.

Wonderlust tip #11

Identifying your love language is one of the healthiest things you can do for yourself and your relationship. It gives you permission to love and be loved in the way you need.

Healthy & Happy Love

Healthy isn't a word we normally use to describe love, but it is the most accurate description of mine. Yes, it is passionate, respectful, supportive, fun, fulfilling, and many other things but ultimately it all falls under the banner of Health. Nestor not only loves me in the way I need to be loved but he makes room in our marriage for the fluctuation of those needs.

This allows me to be myself one hundred percent of the time. He loves and accepts me both at my best and at my worst and he knows how to draw out the best in me on every occasion. Ours is a healthy love where I am free to celebrate my womanhood and my Wonder and to express myself in every area in the most natural way I know how. Now I can truly say I understand what Aretha Franklin meant when singing of the mystery man in her song that made her feel like a natural woman. I believe that's the best description of how Nestor makes me feel.

I share this not to brag, although frankly I waited too long for this type of love to minimize it for anyone. But rather as proof that second chances are sometimes better than first ones and in hopes that you will examine your own marriage or relationship and whether or not you are being loved in the way you need to be.

Health in a marriage or partnership isn't an option; it is a requirement. It's what determines whether your marriage is surviving or thriving. It's what determines the viability of your marriage and finally it's what testifies of your right to be valued and loved in the way you need.

Wonderful-Nes Self-Discovery

1. How many chances have you had in the area of love?

   _____

   _____

2. How do you need to be loved?

   _____

   _____

3. How do you express love?

   _____

   _____

4. Score your current relationship in the following areas by using the following rating system.

    (1) Never
    (2) Occasionally
    (3) Sometimes
    (4) Often
    (5) Always

depleting _____

toxic _____

dangerous _____

identity stripping _____

a poor example to your children _____

narcissistic _____

If you rated a (4) or (5) to any of the above, please explain.

_____

_____

5. Does your spouse or current partner love you the way you need them to love you?

_____

_____

6. Rate the health of your marriage overall, from (1) to (5) with 5 being the healthiest. _____

CHAPTER FIVE

★★★

Wonder Works
-Career, Profession, or Job-

"Choose a job you love and you will never have to work a day in your life".
– Confucius

Ninety thousand hours is the projected time statistics say we will spend working in our lifetime. On average, this is about a third of our life or three thousand seven hundred and fifty days. I'm not sure which one seems longer to you, but when I think of three thousand seven hundred and fifty days it feels quite overwhelming. Whichever way you choose to see it, working looks different for all of us both in nature and in how it unfolds in our day. For some this implies early mornings and yet for others it may mean late nights. When you run your own business, it may include both. Yet, others have built systems that allow their workdays to look like others' vacation days do. One thing is for sure, and that's that work as we know it is continuously being modified by those younger generations that are entering the working age.

Gen Z

What was once a lifestyle that was only accessible to a few is now one that can be created by anyone who puts forth the effort. Phone calls on the beach, virtual meetings while in a five-star hotel in Dubai, sending emails in your pajamas, making money through the sale of products while you sleep, are just some of the ways "work" is being modernized. Generation Z is a prime example of a group that continues to redefine the workspace as we know it.

Between our four children and many nephews who we spend lots of time with, Nestor and I have learned a thing or two about how this particular generation views work. Truth be told, the biggest difference between Gen Z and our Generation (Gen X) is that they view work in a much more pragmatic way than we do. Where previous generations have placed a lot of emphasis on the traditional route of graduating from high school and college, followed by committing to a certain company and/or career for as long as possible, Gen Z has a different approach.

-- Do what you love--

Of course, this is a bit more complicated than it sounds but in theory they are on to something.

In the age of gig economy, influencers, podcasters, gamers, side hustlers, and youtubers choose to take this casual approach when it comes to work to both further their dreams and goals while maximizing their time. This means taking on freelance work such as Door dash, Instacart, Uber, Uber eats, and project-based work amongst many others instead of permanent nine to five jobs. This method of supplementing income at their convenience allows them to concentrate their maximum efforts and energy on developing their true interests.

Inspired by this younger generation, this side-hustle approach to work has caught on across all ages and many choose this approach in order to work on building businesses and chasing those dreams they once thought were no longer an option. Of course, this new perspective on work doesn't happen overnight but is born out of mindset shifts around traditional methods.

Wonderlust tip #12

Evaluate your mindset as it pertains to your current line of work and how you carry it out. If you're not completely satisfied, creating new thinking around old mindsets will help you shift towards more innovative approaches and enhance your productivity.

On the next page are a couple of examples of fixed mindsets that keep us stuck in unproductive patterns as well as opposite phrases to convert those old mindsets to growth ones. Use these to get you started and begin creating personal ones as you move along.

	Fixed	**Growth**
1	Failure defines me and speaks of my inadequacies.	Failure isn't a roadblock; it's a detour on my path to success.
2	Change makes me uncomfortable and triggers my anxiety. I'll stick to what I know.	Adaptability is a necessary skill. I will approach change with curiosity and an open mind to learn new things and become better.
3	Learning requires formal training.	Learning can be experiential, informal, and hands on. There are learning opportunities all around me.
4	I'm only successful if everything is perfect and I reach my goal.	I will celebrate every step in my journey towards my goal. Its not just about the final result but about my effort and the small wins.

The Classroom

When I finally decided to return to college after my years of flying and subsequent dabbling in real estate, I chose to pursue a degree in elementary education. This seemed like an obvious career choice as I had always had a love for small children that was inspired from my grade school experience. The classroom taught me many things, but my biggest lesson was that I didn't belong there.

After three years of long days in a classroom full of six- and seven-year-olds, by the time I would get home, my patience was pretty much non-existent. This posed a problem as my girls were young and required lots of attention from me. Yet after a full day of work, I no longer had that attention to give. It didn't take long before I realized that this wasn't going to be sustainable and so I did what was best for me and my daughters at the time and left the classroom for those that could.

Of course, there was a sense of failure attached to my decision, as no one takes four years out of their life to fully invest in studying something only to later walk out on it. As defeated as I felt at the time and not knowing what was next for me, it was the best decision. Today, I realize this happens so much more than we realize. Had I not taken this leap back then, I might not be where I'm at today doing what I love.

People graduate from careers they never exert all the time and for different reasons. Although it's not ideal and certainly not what we set out to do, a change in careers is simply a fork in the road that can open doors to our best chapter if we have the right mindset in place.

Mary Kay Ash

As mentioned before, I love to read not only for pleasure, but I enjoy access to unlimited amounts of knowledge in any given subject available through books. I place a high value on learning via other people's experiences and am a big proponent for not wasting a great deal of time and effort in creating something that already exists. Or like the famous idiom by Anthony J D'Angelo says, "don't reinvent the wheel". For this reason, I'd much rather follow someone else's recommendation for success and learn as much as I can from their failures and victories along the way if at all possible.

As part of my plan to learn more about business, I decided to read an autobiography by Mary Kay Ash, *Miracles Happen*, the creative genius behind the Mary Kay Ash skin care empire. My first observation was how different the journey to start a business was when Mary Kay launched what began as Mary Kay Cosmetics in 1963 as opposed to now. Just like someone from Generation Z may view Generation X for example, many of the conditions, gender norms, and primarily mindsets that she spoke about seemed outdated and not anything I had ever encountered or adhered to myself. However, there was one fundamental truth she shared that I believe is foundational and transcends generations.

"It took God a long time to get me ready for the job He had for me. All my years of experience, trial, and error, hard work, and disappointment were necessary before I could be guided to form this company."

It's important to note that prior to this cosmetics empire, Mary Kay had a very successful sales career. Yet, it wasn't until her change of career that she felt she had truly come to herself and reached the pinnacle of what she considered her true life's calling to be. Mary Kay's ability to recognize the trials and challenges she had experienced during her career in sales not as a hindrance but as a useful tool, combined with the wisdom to note the culmination of her sales career not as an end but as a beginning, is what catapulted her into great success.

This reframing of mindset was revolutionary in her journey and something we can all learn from. Trials, disappointments, setbacks, challenges, and struggles can all be instruments used to reach the peak of our careers if we allow them to be. But in order to have these drawbacks work --*for us* -- and not against us, we must begin with reframing our mindset. For it is in this shift in perspective that we can begin to view hardships as opportunities to be stretched and not limitations. This is how we use stumbling blocks as ladders to help us climb to the next level of our purpose.

Wonderlust tip #13

Perspective is the key to all things. We might not be able to change our circumstances, but we have complete control over the power we give those circumstances to affect us.

Sailing with Phoenix

Recently, I learned of a man from Oregon named Oliver, who after receiving an unfavorable medical diagnosis where he might eventually face paralysis decided to change his whole life. As we can only imagine, any life-altering news about our health can make us rethink the way we are living and along with that can prompt us to make some drastic changes in the way we are living our life.

Oliver was no different. This diagnosis caused him to come into a realization of many things including how extremely unsatisfied he was with his eleven-year corporate job. He wasn't shy to share his story and how much he hated it. This realization was enough to make him rethink everything about his life and soon after, Oliver quit his job, withdrew his 401K, bought a sailboat, and started to teach himself how to sail. His ultimate goal was to sail the world, without a plan, and to do it with his pet cat Phoenix. Imagine that!

Fast forward three years, during the writing of this book, Oliver has now completed his first long haul voyage across the Pacific Ocean with only Phoenix as a companion. It took him twenty-five days to sail approximately fifteen hundred miles from Oregon to Oahu and he documented the whole journey in real time along the way.

I imagine every step of this endeavor must have been a difficult one. Most people don't wake up one morning and make a plan over breakfast to leave their job, cash out their life savings, and embark on a journey where their life might be put at risk with their pet cat as a sidekick. Most of the time when we hear stories that tend to be so drastic in nature like Oliver and Phoenix, it's one that's been prompted by another incident or series of events. Usually, an occurrence that's so impactful that it causes the person involved to evaluate their life deeply, and consequently, make life-altering choices.

It's moments like these where it becomes clear that the risk of continuing to live life the way we've always lived is bigger than the risk of trying something new.

I can't help but wonder how different our lives would be if we all lived based on this concept. Where we acknowledge that the passive approach we might be taking to life -- in this case in our career -- (but also across the board), is only going to paralyze us in the long run just like Olivers diagnosis. When we dare to venture into our true life's calling or purpose and chase our dream no matter how absurd it might seem, we can rest knowing that though unpredictable, it is still less risky than living a stagnant life.

Misplaced Fear

Most of the time, *fear* is the culprit as to why we decide to play it safe in any area. A natural response to change, *fear* reminds us of all the reasons why we should stick to what we know even if that means living a less than satisfying life. With its matter-of-fact approach, fear will use reasoning to dissuade us from taking any risks. It's important to understand that fear is not just a feeling but a survival mechanism. When we can make this distinction, it becomes easier to separate ourselves from fear and experience it not as a decision maker but as a default internal operating system.

This practical view of fear allows us to see that fear is simply trying to fulfill its role of protection in all circumstances. Once we can recognize that fear in and of itself isn't a deterrent but just a checkpoint on the road to change, then we are more likely to bypass it. As an ever-present emotion that stems from our primitive brain, fear will try to impose itself on every big decision. As such, it is often times misplaced, making us fearful of growth, yet oblivious to the long-term danger that exists in stagnancy.

Understanding the role of fear in our lives is the start to living the life we have always wanted to live and to being in the career we have always desired. The more we understand fear and its function the better prepared we are to both identify and jump on opportunities that lead us closer to our purpose.

Wonderlust tip #14

The more you understand fear, the less power it has over you.

Connect the Dots

As mentioned before, my journey of self-exploration is one that has left no stone unturned. On this quest to evaluate and measure every area of my life for inner fulfillment, I also had to face the obvious dissatisfaction that existed in my career. After ten years in professional development, I was no longer satisfied with what felt like a job that was going nowhere.

Of course, this feeling didn't surface overnight. I had been discontented and feeling unsatisfied for at least three years before actually ever acknowledging it, but fear of not having another plan prolonged my exit from this field and helped me keep the dissatisfaction at bay.

Just like Oliver, it took something significant impacting my life -- in my case a divorce -- to make me reconsider how I was living. It's when we are placed in hard positions that we begin to weigh the consequences of trying something new against the consequences of sticking to what is familiar. For me, it was an obvious choice. I would ride the wave of change I was on to discover the next step in my career in spite of all the unknowns.

Coming off decades worth of being in the education sector in different capacities, it was hard to imagine myself doing anything else. This new era of discovery I was in meant I would have to search deep for my Wonder-Factor and use what seemed like a challenge to step into my next level of purpose. With talents that weren't as obvious as other peoples, all I knew was that my only other passion lied in working with women; something I had no experience in.
Yet, life has a way of always sending us down paths that connect us to purpose.

--Insert God-incidence here--.

Whether we can see the correlation or not, every experience, and every decision we have previously made can serve us in finding and reaching our highest calling if we dare to connect the dots.

Exercising my Wonder Factor

Sometime after the divorce, after some healing and restoration had begun to take place, I found myself wanting to share parts of my journey with other women who might be in the same place I had been just some time before. My idea of doing this was to record a video for social media where I would share little nuggets of truth about my experience and journey in finding my Wonder as a result of my struggles and challenges.

Though exciting to record, hitting the post button felt much different. Fear immediately made its way into my mind and just like it's programmed to do, began its attempt to convince me that I was not qualified to post this video. Reason after reason, it berated me with a laundry list of why this wasn't a good idea.

-No one would want to hear from me after a failed seventeen-year marriage.

-Who was I to want to give anyone advice?

-What made me think I was qualified to talk about any of this?

-Was I even healed enough to have an opinion about anything?

-Who or what was I trying to be?

    The bottom line is fear will always have something to say and it's up to us if we want to give it an audience. Despite all the pushback, I hit post that day. To my surprise it was well received, and I managed to do exactly what I had set out to, which was to empower the next woman who was possibly listening. It turns out the famous proverb by roman poet Virgil, is correct, "Fortune favors the bold".

    That short video led to more videos which eventually led to other projects. Today, I get to do what I am most passionate about despite not having any experience when I started. I help women find their Wonder and since I ventured down this path, I haven't worked a day in my life.

Wonder Works Self- Discovery

1. Are you doing what you love and do you love what you do?

   _____

   _____

2. What is your career and is this what you always dreamt of doing?

   _____

   _____

3. If your current job is not your dream career, what is?

   _____

   _____

4. What Generation are you and what are your beliefs around what work should look like?

   _____

   _____

5. How have your previous experiences prepared you for your dream career or the next step in your current career?

   _____

   _____

6. Do you have any misplaced fear around your career or professional life? If so, what are those?

   _____

   _____

7. What would you do today if you were assured it would be successful?

   _____

   _____

WONDERLUST

CHAPTER SIX

★★★

Wonder-Full
-Financial Health-

"Start where you are, use what you have, do what you can".
-Arthur Ashe

Financial dependence is one of the most popular reasons women stay trapped in relationships they shouldn't be in. As young women, we are taught to look forward to milestones in life such as graduating from college, marriage, motherhood, and other things but financial freedom isn't one. Yes, we are encouraged to go to school and get our degree, but it is my opinion that not enough emphasis is placed on securing our own financial future without the help of a life partner. Building together in a marriage or partnership is the ultimate goal, but as women we should strive to come into a relationship with a preexisting, well established financial foundation. However, we cannot do what we are not taught, so to teach others, we must first learn.

Growing up, my instruction stretched only enough to encourage me to have a savings account. Though certainly a start, this was nowhere near enough to secure a financial future that would allow me to be my own independent person. Job after job and living paycheck to paycheck was my norm. At this pace having any sort of financial independence was never going to happen.

No Alternative

Not surprising when I found myself at the biggest crossroads of my life, it was lack of finances that kept convincing me the only option I had was to stay in the toxic marriage. Bad credit, student loans, and a low paying job, were just a small part of what held me back. I was convinced there was no way I would be able to make it on my own. Not only did I not make enough money to sustain myself and my two daughters, but since I had never taken the role of managing our household finances, I was terrified to think I would have to handle this all on my own. With no assets in my name, to include even the car I drove,

I was convinced there was no alternative but to stay in the marriage.

This fear of not being able to survive on my own kept me stuck in a situation that was completely unhealthy and only continued to get worse. With each day that passed by, I was reminded of how financially impaired I was, and this contributed to all the insecurities I was already dealing with.

When the realization finally hit me that I was losing more by staying in this marriage than by getting out, I made the decision to move forward and take my chances even if this meant financial devastation. Yet, this uncertainty over how I would be able to handle myself financially, continued to haunt me throughout the whole divorce process. I clearly remember sitting with my divorce attorney and the embarrassment of feeling like a four-year-old when he asked me to forecast a budget for my life, post-divorce. I was completely clueless about the amount to allocate for any household expenses because it was nothing I was familiar with. Of course, my case was probably on the extreme side, but typical of someone experiencing financial abuse. Without a doubt, my financial situation at the time, combined with my lack of knowledge as it pertained to finances, was my biggest barrier.

Wonderlust tip #15

Pick up a business or financial literacy book and challenge yourself to make a financial move you have never done. No step is too small. I have included some resources in the *My Favorite Things* section in the back of the book.

God Doesn't Waste a Tear

There's a quote by Frank Peretti I've heard time and time again around my church friends that says, "God doesn't waste a hurt". Rooted in scripture, it's meant to encourage and remind us that everything we go through and the suffering we experience as a result, isn't in vain. Moreover, that same situation that challenged us, but we overcame, can help the next person going through the same or similar situation. In other words, those tears we've shed can serve many purposes, many which are outside ourselves.

Stories shared with us by friends or family who have walked a similar walk to ours, can inspire us and help us find hope. Through their lessons learned, we can become more informed, gain perspective, become encouraged to make hard decisions, or increase our faith in any given situation. It's those candid stories that are shared by others and received by us during our most vulnerable times that have the greatest impact. This is how I was able to find encouragement around my finances when I needed it most.

It was the story of a financial comeback after her divorce that began to inspire hope in me. An afternoon walk at our old place of employment turned into a life learning moment when a friend dared share her journey of pain and subsequent victory. That's where it all began for me. I can clearly remember the feeling of hope rising within me as I listened intently to what she was saying and wondered if the same thing could happen for me.

Her words, simple yet profound, stayed with me for days after. They sparked a belief in me that not only could I stay afloat in this new season -- post divorce -- but I could also potentially create a financial future I could be proud of and most importantly pass that belief on to my girls. Contagious faith was what she gave me that afternoon through her story and is what put me on the path to becoming self-sufficient.

Follow the Yellow Brick Road

If you are a fan of the classic film, *The Wizard of Oz*, then you probably know the yellow brick road began in the heart of the eastern quadrant of

Munchkin Country, in the land of Oz. When Dorothy set out to find the Emerald City and was seeking directions she was instructed to start right where she was at and at the beginning of the yellow brick road. This was the only way to get there and so logically if she stayed on course, she would be sure to reach her destination.

The story goes on to tell us about the journey and all the characters she encountered along the way, eventually resulting in her reaching the Emerald City. Broken down into more practical terms, Dorothy followed a very basic concept to reach her destination.

-Start where you're at – The beginning of the yellow brick road

-Use what you have – The ruby red slippers

-Do what you can – Meet, befriend, and save the scarecrow, the tinman, and the cowardly lion

Though she may have wanted to cut corners, take another road, or borrow someone else's possessions to get to the Emerald City faster, this was the only road available for her to take. As little or ill equipped as she must have felt for this journey with only the ruby slippers as an asset, these were all she would ever need to make it to the Emerald city for her particular cause and purpose. Once she stepped out in faith, everything else would fall into place including who she would meet, the support she would find and the lessons she would learn along the way.

It bears mentioning that parallel to the infamously swirling yellow brick road, there was a red road. No one ever mentions this one because it wasn't Dorothy's path. Perhaps it led to the same destination with different pit stops along the way or maybe it led somewhere completely different, but all the audience is left to know is that this one wasn't for her to take.

Very similar to Dorothy, we all have our own yellow brick road of sorts in life that is unique to each of us. Comparatively there always seems to be someone we know on a red road next to us in what appears to be a much smoother and faster route and with more access to different resources. Yet, it's important to keep in mind that if we want to reach our destination there is no swapping of roads.

The road to financial independence or self-sufficiency is one that is available to us all and begins right where we are at. Though the journey will look different for each of us, it's important that we trust the right people and resources are already in place waiting for us to bump into them en-route. It's normal to think we don't have all the things we need to start our journey to our individual Emerald City, but my observation has been that just like the characters in the movie, the only thing we need in order to begin is heart, courage, and a made-up mind to do so. The rest always has a way of working itself out.

If you have any doubt that you too can follow this same concept to reach the level of financial independence that you're seeking, then perhaps you need to evaluate your circle and surround yourself with other women who are walking their own yellow brick road and passing on contagious faith in the process. We will discuss this in more depth in the following chapter.

Notary Kiosk

One of my favorite examples of someone using the *Start where you're at, Use what you have, Do what you can,* method is of an ex-coworker turned friend. From the moment I met Sara, I knew there was something unique about her. She possesses an audacity and boldness in dealing with situations that are many times misunderstood, but necessary when stepping into a new endeavor. Her blatant disregard for conventional thought coupled with her lack of fear of failure made it obvious that it was only a matter of time before she would reach her dreams.

Throughout the time we worked together and even a couple of years after, I witnessed her taking incremental steps towards her financial freedom. Always looking for ways to get better, Sara would take advantage of any opportunity presented to her in order to increase her knowledge and capacity. Her life and accomplishments are proof that we don't get ahead by luck but rather by hard work.

I am a big believer that God meets us at the point of our effort so it's imperative that we do our part so that He can do His. In fact, it has been my experience that He not only meets us but doubles our effort in the way only some-kind-of Wonderful could. I believe this is what Sara experienced. With seventy-three dollars in her bank account and a heart full of hope she launched her dream business; **Notary Kiosk**.

Sara *started where she was at* by evaluating her skills and what she could contribute to society and her community. Being the outgoing person that she is and seeing a need for a notary that could service the Latinx community in a bilingual fashion, she decided to become a notary public for the state of Florida. In the age of multiple streams of income, this began as a small side hustle that put extra cash in her pocket but soon after evolved in potential. Where other people obtain their notary public seal and stick to the conventional approach of providing a general service, Sara had bigger plans and came up with an innovative way to expand the services she was currently providing.

Out of a desire to do more, Notary Kiosk was born. It began as an idea for a mobile - on duty - notary that also had a fixed location. Little by little she continued to flush out her vision and after saving some dollars and *using what she had* to make this vision a reality, she purchased a trailer that she could restore and use as a permanent yet mobile location.

Sara was on the verge of making her dreams a reality. After a successful restoration of what is now her mobile office and creating a menu of services that offers *all those things she can do*, Sara successfully opened her business. She is now completely self-employed, scaling her business and building her own financial portfolio. She found a way to create financial independence by using the *start where you are, use what you have, do what you can* method. Below is an example of what this method looked like for her.

Start where you are:

-Evaluating her skills as well as the needs of the community and how she could use her skills to service them in an innovative way

-Going through the process of becoming a certified notary public in the state of Florida

Use what you have:

-Started as a side hustle to save money to eventually purchase her trailer

-Social media as advertising of her services

-Purchasing a trailer for her vision of a mobile notary (we come to you) with a permanent location (annex to the courthouse building)

Do what you can:

-Bilingual notary services

-Interpreting services

-Process services & Legal Courier

-Virtual Offices & Court Hearing Zoom Call setups

Wonderlust tip #16

God meets us at the point of our effort. Do your part so that He can in turn do His. Start with what you have, and in due time the next steps will be revealed.

Joy of Buying a Couch

In a time where information about any subject is just a click away, it behooves us to educate ourselves in all those areas that we aren't proficient in; especially if it's an area where we are experiencing a challenge. There are countless free communities, videos, masterclasses, and books amongst many other things, which are filled with useful knowledge we can begin using immediately on our journey to financial success. These are the exact resources I took advantage of when I found myself post-divorce attempting to build a financial future. It didn't happen overnight but by applying the strategies I learnt I was able to:

-Negotiate with creditors

-Restore my credit

-Raise my credit score

-Make small purchases --all on my own—

-Buy my own car

-Pay off credit card debt

-Apply for and obtaining elite credit cards

-Invest in the stock market

-Open and max out a Roth IRA

-Open Roth IRAs for my daughters

-Invest in crypto

Not too bad for someone with no prior knowledge of anything financial. Using the available resources, I was able to start right where I was at and work my way up to creating the financial independence I was seeking and longed to pass on to my girls. Again, it didn't happen overnight but in retrospect I'm glad it didn't as this allowed me to appreciate my growth much more than if it had.

I still remember towards the beginning of my financial independence journey the immense anxiety I felt as I applied for a thousand-dollar credit line at the furniture store. This was my first attempt at what I considered a "big" purchase on my own at the time. My daughters were excited about a small makeover project for our living room. This would require a new couch, which also happened to be the biggest ticket item on our list and crucial to the change we were seeking. Our couch at the time was a major eye-sore and replacing it would give that fresh new feeling we were trying to create.

With the divorce still fresh, I wanted nothing other than to be able to provide this for my daughters, as proof to them and myself that we could make it on our own.

The longest fifteen minutes of my life was waiting for a response to see if they had approved me for the loan. I had already begun to prepare the speech in my head where I would pretend I wasn't feeling defeated when they didn't approve us and proceed to tell the girls how the old couch wasn't that bad after all. To my surprise our salesperson came back with a resounding yes! This was the first time I felt like we would be okay. Who would have thought a couch could bring so much joy and assurance?

I too, *started where I was, used what I had, and did what I could.* That was just the start of my financial independence journey. Today, I find myself grateful for the hard moments that strengthened me, the insights gained, the people willing to guide me, and the ability to pass the knowledge I've learned on to my daughters.

Being financially independent and savvy is nonnegotiable and crucial to us as women. Now more than ever, we need to be aware of our individual skills and know how to leverage those skills, connections, and resources to obtain additional streams of income and ultimately create financial independence.

Wonder-full Self-Discovery

1. Do you consider yourself to be financially independent?

   _____

   _____

2. What is the one thing that lack of finances stops you from doing?

   _____

   _____

3. Complete the following to determine where you are on your journey to financial independence:

   Start where you're at:

   _____

   Use what you have:

   _____

   Do what you can:

   _____

4. What is your next big financial move?

   _____

   _____

CHAPTER SEVEN

★★★

Wonder Land
-Friendships & Community-

"Walk with the dreamers, the believers, the courageous, the cheerful, the planners, the doers, the successful people with their heads in the clouds and their feet on the ground"
– Wilferd Peterson

January of 2024 I had the opportunity to launch a social media spotlight series called *Wonder in your Woman Wednesdays.* It was a space where every day sheroes -- oftentimes unnoticed -- got recognized for their contributions. These weekly highlights were meant to applaud women who are making a difference in their communities through what they do and changing lives in the process. Every story that was featured spoke of a woman who was living out her passion and working towards her dreams in a bold and unapologetic fashion. With each woman I had the opportunity to feature I found myself completely Wonderstruck!

Advocates, pastors, masseuses, nonprofit founders, podcasters, violinists, financial consultants, authors, bakers, aestheticians, were just some of the trailblazers I had the opportunity of featuring. While highlighting their greatest achievements, and entrepreneurial journeys was the focus, getting to know the *"why"* behind each of their stories was just as important as the work they were each carrying out. It is in the stories of those pre-success days that each of these women had found their Wonder and received the stamina for their cause.

When we surround ourselves with women who are operating in their calling it can be both electrifying and contagious. Oftentimes their passion and their intense devotion to the thing they do can almost feel palpable. This is the type of community we should always strive to be surrounded by, all while recognizing that the landscape of our relationships is an ever-changing one.

Wonderland Characters

At any given point in our lives, our circle is made up of an array of friends, family, acquaintances, co-workers and others that we are directly and indirectly influenced by. With the exception of a select few, this group will continue to evolve overtime. New people will come in and some that we never thought would leave, exit the Wonderland of our life.

Like characters in a play some have permanent roles while others complete their scene and exit the stage of our life never to be seen again. It is important to differentiate the role of each character in our life so that we can have clarity about who the leads are, who has a supporting role, and to properly identify the extras. This can help specifically when we consider who and what we are being influenced by. When we accept that the panorama of our relationships is ever evolving, it becomes much easier to surrender to the reality that people come and people go and either way it all works together for our good.

Wonderlust tip #17

Passion is transferable and so is apathy. Mind the company you keep.

Lead Characters

Growing up, my sister Barbie loved to watch soap operas. Dallas, All My Children, and Santa Barbara were just some of her favorites that I can recall. Although I wasn't nearly as committed to these novelas as her, I was familiar enough to know who the lead actors were and the story line that was developing, especially when it was a juicy one. There were always a couple of different story lines taking place all at once, but as you would expect there was only one star in the show. Everything seemed to revolve around this one person with common story lines surrounding a love interest and a villain. After all, there wouldn't be much of a story if there wasn't someone to hate on. Whether liked by the audience or not these lead characters carried the main plot of the show, and their role was undeniable.

Every afternoon Barbie would rush home from school to make sure and catch the drama-filled show that was sure to leave her facing a cliff hanger until the next day. Though I wouldn't always join her in this pursuit, whenever I did, I could successfully identify everyone's role within just a couple of minutes.

Lead characters are easy to identify because they are the ones with many lines and lots of influence. Whether in a soap opera or real life, lead characters are usually made up of significant others, adult children, close family members, or sometimes friends. Those principal characters play a significant role in the protagonist's life. Their opinion counts more than everyone else's and it's usually evident by the way the main character responds to them.

When it comes to our personal life stage, we have complete control over who has access and for this reason, it is important that we carefully vet who we allow in these positions of influence in our life. This person or person(s) who usually have unlimited access to our time, attention, and many times resources can indirectly influence us towards success or failure.

It's no surprise that once an unhealthy relationship comes to an end, the lead character who may have been struggling in some areas of life suddenly begins to soar as they never had before. For this reason, the lead characters in our life are so important.

Supporting Role

It isn't unheard of that someone who starts off being a lead character in our life passes on to a supporting role with time. This can occur due to changes in status of relationships, distance, and any other number of reasons. These people, though still impactful, are more limited in terms of the access they have to us and the influence they carry.

Many times, this group includes people such as siblings, parents, close friends, and business partners to name a few. Supporting characters can also play a vital role in helping us to reach our goals and offering wise counsel but from more of a distance. As the name suggests, their role is to support, encourage, and give input when asked.

There is a popular saying by American novelist Harper Lee that states, "You can choose your friends, but you can't choose your family". Though this is true, it's in our best interest to recognize that though family can't be chosen we are still in control over how much energy, attention, and time we give them. It's important to note this, as many struggle with toxic family members and their automation into a supporting role in their lives.

Many times, we can be made to feel guilty when we begin to raise boundaries specifically as it pertains to family. Yet, what we should keep in mind is that boundaries are not walls meant to keep those close to us out, but rather standards meant to make sure our limits are being honored, and our peace is being protected. Those with our best interest in mind will observe any boundaries we put in place and will understand this isn't personal. It is only people who have been benefiting from us not having any boundaries or standards that will have an issue when we decide to set these in place.

Other supporting characters in our lives might include mentors, coaches, church family and others we have become close to throughout the years. In the same manner, it is up to us as the lead character to decide the proximity of those relationships and how much influence they will have on us.

Our goal as women, at all times, should be to surround ourselves with people who are contributing to build us into the best version of ourselves. As the name states, *supporting characters'* roles are to provide us with words of wisdom, encouragement, or council from a place of having our best interest in mind. Those we spend time with and lend an ear to will indirectly influence whether we continue to grow or whether our growth is stunted. Part of keeping those supporting character roles in our life viable and healthy is intentionally and periodically evaluating our relationships to measure if those in close proximity are:

-pushing us to become better

-encouraging us to reach higher, or

-inspiring us to strive for more

If they aren't doing any one of these things, then they may inadvertently be encouraging us to live a mediocre life.

This evaluation should apply to every relationship we have, including the oldest or longest ones. Specifically, because the longer someone has known us, the more likely they are to want to cling to old versions of us. Subconsciously, those who do this might be encouraging mediocrity because it is the version of us they are familiar with and fear losing.

Extras

As a young adult, in between my flight attendant days and going back to school to pursue my degree, there was a time I wanted to be an actress. I believe I mentioned this tendency to be a *Jill of all trades* in an earlier chapter. This was one of those times. Anyway, I digress.

The closest I ever got to that dream was working as a stand in for Demi Moore's movie, Striptease, and a couple of "extra" roles here and there that were, well, insignificant. I remember being on set once as an extra at a rock quarry location for a music video. I was one among what seemed like a hundred other extras who were inside a school bus with crazy make-up and orange clothes, instructed to dance to the tune of this rock band who were the stars of the show.

It was quite exciting at the time and though the role was of little if any importance, I did get my kicks out of being able to say that I was in it and wondered if my face would somehow be amongst the ones highlighted in the video. It was a whole day's worth of work, and I can distinctively remember getting paid one hundred dollars for my efforts. I don't recall ever seeing this video on any sort of media after that day.

This experience explains exactly what extras are. They are people with insignificant roles or opinions in our lives trying to get airtime. These characters are often made up of co-workers, business acquaintances, family friends, ex-wives, ex-husbands, or all other exes, and a number of other individuals whose input means nothing in our lives in the grand scheme of things. When we observe the role of an extra closely, we realize that they are simply in the stage of our life to take up space for a moment in time. Yet, many times as the lead character we might get caught up with their presence and begin to give them room to act or a voice.

The primary attribute of an extra which we have to keep in mind at all times, is that extra's never have any lines. When we come across an extra in our life who wants to give opinions or input, it is imperative that we remind ourselves of their role. Doing this will help us refrain from wasting time and energy on something or someone whose role and/or opinions have little to no value.

For clarity's sake let's look at this in terms of value and analyze how much of it we place on other characters. Where those in lead roles might be given the energy of a nine or ten in value, a supporting role might receive anywhere from a six to an eight, for example. This means that those who would be considered extras should be given the energy of a one or two at best.

Upon going through the process of evaluating relationships as I mentioned before, or when trying to determine the involvement of someone in any given situation this is a good approach to take as it will help clarify the voices we are listening to. This is also a good way to self-check for any characters we are giving room to that don't need to be there anymore. And as the popular term in production goes, once their part is done, they should be instructed to *exit stage right*.

Wonderlust tip #18

Categorize your community based on lead characters, supporting roles, and extras. Consider how much of your time and zeal you are investing in any of those people at any given point in time. Make adjustments as necessary.

Collaboration not Competition

Women who operate in this range of categorizing roles might find they have a small inner circle. This process of categorization isn't meant to isolate, but rather to assure the highest quality in our circle of influence. It has been my experience that the more intimate your circle is, the more space you have for clear thinking and making decisions out of authenticity and not influence. After all, it's not about the amount of input and opinions that we have, but about the quality. This protection of our time, space, and energy in turn allows us to attract only the most like-minded individuals into our Wonderland.

Authenticity invites authenticity and the more we can operate out of a place where we are honoring our true principles, the more people of similar character will come into our circle. These types of people understand the fundamental truth of collaboration not competition.

Where competition has its place in sports or sales, for example, and is fueled by one general prize or place of recognition, collaboration is the opposite. Collaboration understands there is room enough for all of us to win and plenty of opportunities to go around. It also acknowledges that dimming someone else's light isn't going to make ours shine brighter.

Push & Pull

There's an adage in Spanish that translates to, "Tell me who you spend time with, and I'll tell you who you are". It sounds a lot better in its original language, but the general meaning it invokes has an equivalent in most languages. A similar one is a quote by motivational speaker Jim Rohn, "You are the average of the five people you spend the most time with".

In the same sentiment as the first, this quote really inspires reflection about who those five people we spend the most time with are (for each of us individually) and what that median says about us. It should be our goal to surround ourselves with dreamers, believers, doers, go-getters, and the likes of individuals like this as to assure ourselves that what it reflects about us is positive.

When considering the five people we spend the most time with (that number might differ slightly for you), we should also acknowledge their success in comparison to ours. Now before you get the wrong idea let me explain. The famous saying by President Theodore Roosevelt says, "Comparison is the thief of Joy" and his words couldn't be more accurate.

However, when done for the right reasons, comparison can be a great motivator and even a source of inspiration. In the case I'm trying to make this comparison is solely for the purpose of what I call Push & Pull.

To simplify this same example of being the average of the people you spend the most time with, consider the four closest people to you. Ensure that you have at least two people that are doing better than you in any given area and two people that need to catch up with where you're at. This creates the perfect amount of push and pull. It's in this manner that you can be sure you are both growing and forcing yourself to get to your next level to reach those doing better than you, as well as giving of your current knowledge and experience to someone who needs to catch up to where you're at.

-We Push ourselves to become better as we are inspired and mentored by those ahead of us (Persons 1 & 2 in the graphic)

-We Pull up those that are trying to catch up to our current level of knowledge and know-how by teaching them what we know. (Persons 3 & 4 in the graphic)

If and when anyone of those four people in our Push & Pull circle outgrows their position, we should actively seek to replace someone in that spot in order to keep the momentum going. This guarantees that we are constantly in the middle position of this group and therefore being challenged to do and accomplish more as well as challenging those who need it.

If you find yourself being the smartest, most advanced, or most successful person in your circle it is imperative that you make some adjustments to your circle so that you can remain in a constant state of growth. It's In this way that we maximize our inner circle in a way that is beneficial to all. We Push and we Pull.

This is the real meaning of being the average of the people we spend the most time with and what we should strive to attain. Using this method ensures that we all win and helps us not only find our Wonder but be the catalyst for someone else to be able to find theirs.

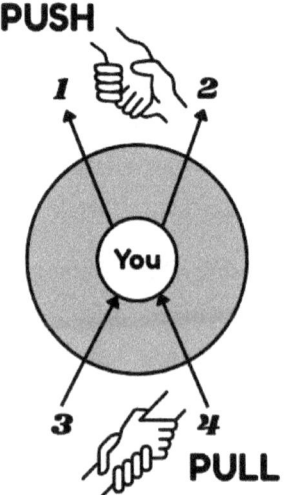

Wonderland Self- Discovery

1. In the screen play of your life who are the following characters?

   _____

   _____

- Lead Roles

  A.   C.

  B.   D.

- Supporting Roles

  A.   C.

  B.   D.

- Extras

  A.   C.

  B.   D.

2. Are you giving the Extra's in your life room to act or a voice?

   _____

   _____

3. Who are you collaborating with and in what?

   _____

   _____

4. Who would you like to collaborate with and in what?

   _____

   _____

5. Are you in competition with anyone and why?

   _____

   _____

6. The quote says, "You are the average of the five people you spend the most time with". Who are those people in your life?

   1.   4.
   2.   5.
   3.

   What does it say about you?

   _____

   _____

7. Who are you pushing yourself to be more like? Or who Pushes you to the next level?

   _____

   _____

8. Who are you Pulling up to their next level through your encouragement and experience?

   _____

   _____

WONDERLUST

CHAPTER EIGHT

★★★

Wonderstruck

*A prayer for wonder invites God to begin
transforming us from the inside out.
– Margaret Feinberg*

Wonderstruck is defined as experiencing a sudden feeling of awed delight or wonder. Moments like this don't happen every day so when they do, we certainly remember them. That first look at our children, a stunning bride walking down the aisle, the vast ocean from the balcony of a cruise ship, or mountain peaks so high they are covered by clouds or snow are just some of the moments that can leave us gasping for air. The motive for our admiration is almost always something outside of us that when we witness can take up permanent residence in our minds. Popping up every so often, the memories come back to offer us hope and somehow manage to refill us with the same charm we once felt when first witnessing it. Once we are wonderstruck it never leaves us.

However, this isn't the only type of wonderstruck that exists. There are countless wonders in the world waiting to be discovered every day but unless we become wonder seekers we will miss them. Everyday encounters with people and things around us have the potential of leaving us just as wonderstruck as for example, star gazing can. This more practical form of being wonderstruck can happen in a casual conversation or through a shared story and has the ability to impact and transform us in much the same way.

The Great Pyramid of Giza

In 2021 Nestor and I had the pleasure of visiting one of the original ancient wonders of the world along with our kids. As the only remaining structure still standing, from the original seven wonders list, the Great Pyramid of Giza in Egypt did not disappoint. Our guide, Dalia -- the best Egyptologist in Cairo -- gave us a scholarly lesson on the three pyramids in the Giza Plateau, the pharaohs they were built for, and their construction. By the end of the tour, we were completely wonderstruck!

It's one thing to read about the great pyramid in books or to see pictures of it but standing at its base and witnessing the engineering and the size of this structure that is still standing 4,500 years later is just mind boggling. Had I not witnessed it myself I would have never understood the magnitude of its giant boulders and how they could possibly form this perfect triangle skyrocketing into the skies for almost 480 feet. It's hard to fathom that after thousands of years this structure could survive all the elements it has faced since its conception.

For those that have visited, I'm sure you would agree there's a certain transference of belief that takes place when you are able to see it with your own eyes and as such, attest to a civilization that is long gone but still very much alive in the remains of this structure.

Though the other ancient wonders of the world were probably just as majestic as the Great Pyramid of Giza, I submit that it's hard to be as wonderstruck by something we've never seen as it is to be by a structure that still speaks for itself. This is the nature of all wonder-filled things. They exist independent of an interpreter or facilitator, and don't require a formal introduction to give them credibility. They don't need a precursor. They simply are.

Wonderlust tip #19

**We don't have to be convinced of wonder.
Wonder makes a statement all on its own.**

Transference of Belief

Being wonderstruck begins with the transference of belief. The moment we move from having no faith to believe *for* something or in something, to complete assurance of the manifestation of that same thing is when this transference happens. Transference of belief always has a source or initiator which serves as proof of an outcome and in turn creates the perfect opportunity to move us from an incredulous state to one of certainty.

TRANSFER OF BELIEF

For instance, the Great Pyramid of Giza's presence alone has the ability to create credence in the eye of the beholder and can consequently leave them wonderstruck. This is a pretty straight forward example. This structure that has been spoken about for over four millennia and is there for people around the world to witness, stands tall and proud and again speaks for itself. Undoubtedly, there is no room for questioning the reality of this structure and whether it's survived the years and any hostile environment it may have been put up against.

The source or initiator is the pyramid itself, and the transference of belief happens at witnessing its existence and resilience throughout the years. This same logic applies to all those things around us that have the potential of impacting us and leaving us in awe through the process of transferring belief. If the source can speak for itself then it has the ability to create pockets of opportunity for transformation and to leave us wonderstruck.

In the previous chapters, I shared my personal examples and stories of how I navigated different challenges and turned them into victories. Resilience, survival, and growth were the common themes throughout. My hope is that you as the reader were able to pick up on these, as well as how I managed to keep standing despite those moments where I believed I couldn't. Life after divorce, finding love in the second chance, financial independence, career changes and purpose were just some of the topics I shared in hopes of transferring belief and creating those pockets for transformation so that you could believe for the same outcome.

Wonderlust tip #20

Transferring Belief is the passing on of certainty which creates opportunities for real transformation beyond the inspiration of the moment.

Borrowed Belief

It's important to note that the belief you might be experiencing right now might feel like a borrowed one and not totally yours. This is a common occurrence, as borrowed belief from the initiator is many times what sustains us until we are able to create our own. We might borrow strength, resilience, confidence, courage, possibility or a slew of other things all with the intention of achieving a desired outcome. Not only is borrowed belief normal, but it's exactly what you need right now to begin driving your behavior and actions and creating the results you long to see.

Wonderlust tip #21

Borrowed Belief serves as a placeholder until you reach a place where you are able to establish your own.

My hope is that as you read through the pages of this book, you were wonderstruck and as such inspired to want for more in all the different areas of your own life. This might require you to go back and re-read a chapter and dwell longer in those pockets of transformation available to you, so that you experience a time of honest self-reflection and subsequently, change. My intention is that the message of **Wonderlust** would linger long past your reading of the same and would serve as a reminder that this wonder-filled life is available for you too.

Being wonderstruck doesn't happen by chance. As we noted before, coincidences don't exist. If you came across this book, then perhaps this is your sign to seek more.

Be a Wonder seeker.
Be Wonderstruck.

Wonderstruck Self- Discovery

1. What was the last thing in nature that you were Wonderstruck by and why?

   _____

   _____

2. Recall a time when you experienced a transference of belief. What was it and who was the initiator?

   _____

   _____

3. Are you borrowing belief from any of the stories in Wonderlust? If so, what are you borrowing and what are you believing for?

   _____

   _____

4. Each chapter of Wonderlust serves as a pocket of transformation available for you to have the same or similar outcome. Did you experience a transfer of belief in any chapter and what was it?

_____

_____

5. Will you be re-reading a chapter? Which one?

_____

_____

WONDERLUST

CONCLUSION

★★★

Wonder Seeker

The biggest adventure you can take is to live the life of your dreams.

– Oprah Winfrey

On our travels with our now young adult children, Nestor and I always try to incorporate a level of adventure. Not only for their pleasure but because we're also fans of exciting feats. Well, more him really. We look forward to at least one extreme sport adventure per trip which usually winds up being a conversation point for the duration of our journey.

Amongst the adventures we've been able to do, has been riding an air balloon at sunrise over the

Nile river, paragliding over the mountains in Colombia, zip lining through the forest in Mexico, white water rafting and rock climbing in Costa Rica, hiking through the Amazon Rainforest of Ecuador as well as rafting and taking a dip in the same. These are just some of the many adventures that will never be forgotten. Besides doing all this for fun, our goal is to encourage our children to live freely, be explorers, and to do those things that make their hearts race in exhilaration. If they incorporate these principles, not only in traveling but in every aspect of life, they are sure to find inner fulfillment.

Usually, leading up to one of our adventures, we begin to question whether or not we should be doing it and start to consider all the "what if's". There's a certain level of intimidation that can creep up from not knowing what to expect. Yet, what causes us to get past these feelings of uncertainty is what we've learned from past experiences about the nature of trying something new. These have taught us that every new challenge comes with its own roller coaster of emotions that if we manage to keep in check, can lead us to our highest level of accomplishment.

Fear, anxiety, anticipation, excitement, and elation, being the most common one's, followed by a sense of achievement and gratefulness which is only felt once the adventure is complete. The experience usually leaves us not only Wonderstruck but teaches us that great things do indeed lie on the other side of fear. And most importantly, if we don't challenge what's familiar and courageously step out to do those things that make us uncomfortable, we might be denying ourselves our biggest win!

Without a doubt the journey of self-exploration and inner fulfillment is the most adventurous journey we can ever take. Herein, we find mountains high and valleys low of pure wonder that have remained hidden awaiting the moment that a wonder seeker like you will discover it.

May **Wonderlust** be your biggest and most profound journey yet, leading you to your truest and most fulfilled self.

WONDERLUST

Acknowledgments

I never intended to write this book. In fact, after writing my first book I promised myself that I would never do it again. Of course, G-d had other plans –doesn't He always--?!?

And so here I am once again, but this time I have made no such promises to myself. I realize that I am a message conveyor. I write because I have a message to share and so long as life continues to entrust a message to me, the only promise I make is to share it.

Of course, writing a book is no easy feat. It takes time, energy, patience, sacrifice, other people's help, and did I mention time? The ones that feel the burden the most are those closest to you as they're the ones that have to make the biggest sacrifice. Less time spent together, writing on days when you're supposed to be relaxing with everyone else, late evenings, all just to get it done. So, the biggest thanks go to those that have waited on the sideline for me to finish.

My ladybugs Sky and Rain. Never complaining --not once-- but instead rooting me on with enthusiasm and encouraging me with your uplifting words. It's because you believe in me and think that I can do anything (well, almost anything) that I am really able to do it. Your belief in me gives me strength and courage and motivates me to strive for more. All of it is for you!

Life doesn't stop because you're writing a book. Theres still a house to take care of, dinners to make, laundry to do and a whole lot of anxiety when things are in disarray and you're finally on a good writing streak that you don't want to break away from. Mami, gracias por siempre estar presente para ayudarme. Ya sea en los quehaceres de la casa para que yo pueda terminar algo que tengo pendiente o estando disponible para hablar y darme consejos cuando me siento frustrada. Es por tu presencia, tu apoyo, y por tus palabras de ánimo que pude terminar de escribir el libro tan rápido. No sabes cuánta ayuda eres para mí.

To the one that has been present from the beginning, my sister Barbie. We shared the Disney trips, the tuna sandwiches, Circus World, and the soap operas amongst so many other things. We also shared a father that was peculiar to say the least but who also instilled this love for wander lusting in both of us. Thank you for loving me through all the different phases of my life, and for standing by me when no one else did, and being patient as I found my wonder.

Thank you, mother-in-love, Maria, for helping with the edits and proof reading. You didn't

Acknowledgments

have to, but you did. You were also the first to read this finished work in its entirety. Your support is so appreciated.

A huge thank you to all those women in my life that have been examples when I've needed them. Examples of strength, bravery, humility and badassery!

And finally, to my Wonderful-NES. My retroactive love, my baby boo. The one who allowed me to be my truest self in all aspects and still loved me. Thank you for everything you do. Not only in helping me put **Wonderlust** together but in encouraging me every step of the way in all things. You love me perfectly and none of it works without you. Thank you for inspiring me to search for the Wonder in my Woman every day!

WONDERLUST

Notes

"Men go abroad to wonder at the heights of mountains, at the huge waves of the sea, at the long courses of the rivers, at the vast compass of the ocean, at the circular motions of the stars, and they pass by themselves without wondering". - St Augustine

All things proclaim the existence of God. -Napolean Bonaparte

Dr Seuss – *"Oh the places you'll go"*

"We are not human beings having a spiritual experience; we are spiritual beings having a human experience." – Pierre Tielhard De Chardin

Coincidence: *a remarkable concurrence of events or circumstances without apparent casual connection* Webster's Dictionary

Wonder is the beginning of Wisdom -Socrates

"*There is no greater gift you can give or receive than to honor your calling. It's why you were born. And how you become most truly alive."* – Oprah Winfrey

"The graveyard is the richest place on earth, because it is here that you will find all the hopes and dreams that were never fulfilled". - Myles Munroe

"Life can only be understood backwards, but it must be lived forwards". – Soren Kierkegaard

Love is patient, love is kind. It does not envy, it does not boast, it is not proud. (1 Corinthians 13:4)

Choose a job you love and you will never have to work a day in your life. – Confucius

"Don't reinvent the wheel". – Anthony J. D'Angelo

"It took God a long time to get me ready for the job He had for me. All my years of experience, trial, and error, hard work, and disappointment were necessary before I could be guided to form this company." – Mary Kay Ash

"Fortune favors the bold" – Virgil

Start where you are, use what you have, do what you can. -Arthur Ashe

"God doesn't waste a hurt" – Frank Peretti

Vidor, King, et al. The Wizard of Oz. [Film]. Metro-Goldwyn-Mayer, 1939

Notes

"Walk with the dreamers, the believers, the courageous, the cheerful, the planners, the doers, the successful people with their heads in the clouds and their feet on the ground" – Wilferd Peterson

"You can choose your friends, but you can't choose your family" – Harper Lee

"Comparison is the thief of joy" – President Theodore Roosevelt

Tell me who you spend time with, and I'll tell you who you are. – Don Quijote De La Mancha, Miguel De Cervantes

"Dime con quién andas y te diré quién eres" – Don Quijote De La Mancha, Miguel De Cervantes

"You are the average of the five people you spend the most time with" – Jim Rohn

A prayer for wonder invites God to begin transforming us from the inside out – Margaret Feinberg

"The biggest adventure you can take is to live the life of your dreams" – Oprah Winfrey

WONDERLUST

Index

Introduction
Dr. Seuss, Road trips, Circus World, Travel, Wanderlust, Wonder seeking, Wonder Woman, Family Manager, Wonder, fairytales, essence, family manager, wonder-factor

Chapter 1
Some-Kind-of-Wonderful, Multiple Intelligences, Howard Gardner, Existentialism, faith, catholic, spiritual, Godincidences, Highest level

Chapter 2
Wonder, Wander, Mind Wandering, Wander Women, Wonder Women, Contagious, Costume Contest, Sheroes, Root Mindset

Chapter 3
Purpose, Zone of Wonder, Wonder Factor, Bridge, Puzzles, Retrospection, Connection, Admission Personal Growth, Imaginary Boots

Chapter 4
Wonderful, Second Chance, Unexpected Wins, Race, Strawberries, Healthy Love, Happy Love, Retroactive Love, Love Languages, Loss of Identity

Chapter 5
Wonder Works, Gen Z, Fixed Mindset, Growth Mindset, Careers, Mary Kay Ashe, Sailing, Fear, Connect the Dots, Work

Chapter 6
Wonder-full, Finances, Self-Sufficiency, Stories, Belief, Contagious Faith, Yellow Brick Road, Red Road, Emerald City, Heart, Courage, Mind, Notary Kiosk, Financial Independence, Credit, Invest, Stock Market, Roth IRA's, Couch

Chapter 7
Wonderland, Relationships, Characters, Lead Roles, Supporting Roles, Extras, Soap Opera, Push, Pull, Collaboration, Competition, Comparison

Chapter 8
Wonderstruck, Ancient Wonder, Giza, Pyramid, Egypt, Transference of Belief, Source, Initiator, Pockets, Transformation, Borrowed Belief, Self-Reflection, Change
Conclusion Wonder Seeker, Adventure, Explorers, Inner Fulfillment

My Favorite Things
&
Recommended Reading

Multiple Intelligences Test – Howard Gardner

https://www.psychologytoday.com/us/tests/iq/multiple-intelligences-learning-style-test

The 5 Love Languages by Gary Chapman

(You Make Me Feel Like) A Natural Woman – Song by Aretha Franklin 1968

Miracles Happen by Mary Kay Ash

Instagram & Youtube @ sailing_with_phoenix

Secrets of the Millionaire Mind by T. Harv Eker

The Richest Man in Babylon by George S. Clason

Your First Million by Arlan Hamilton

The Power of Positive Thinking by Norman Vincent Peale

Refined in the Flame by Rosie Jensing

The Wizard of Oz [Film] Metro-Goldwyn-Mayer, 1939

WONDERLUST

Wonderlust Tips

Wonderlust tip #1

Take a multiple intelligence quiz to learn more about the ways you are smart. I am including additional information about the quiz in *the My Favorite Things* section in the back of the book.

Wonderlust Tip #2

If Some-Kind-of-Wonderful isn't a part of your everyday life, look for ways to develop this area.

Wonderlust tip #3

Take the Wonderlust "Best Version of Yourself" inventory to check for your level of harmony in each area of life. This is available as a downloadable format and printable version in the free book bonuses when you visit wonderinyourwoman.com.

Wonderlust tip #4

Unresolved issues are contagious and the perfect incubator for creating *Wander Women*. Don't be the wrong type of superhero. We are *Wonder Women not Wander Women!*

Wonderlust tip #5

Practice incorporating the Wonderlust mindsets which affirm the belief that life is happening for you not to you. These are available as a downloadable format and printable version in the free book bonuses when you visit wonderinyourwoman.com.

Wonderlust tip #6

As the essence of our gifting, Wonder, can take on a different shape depending on the phase of life we are in. The outlet might not always look the same, but its core faculties are always there.

Wonderlust tip #7

Sometimes, the only way out is through. We can't avoid the feelings that come from connecting the pieces but its only through the connection that the disarray begins to make sense and takes on order.

Wonderlust tip #8

It's in personal growth that the wonder factor we may have been oblivious to becomes evident. This part is ongoing and crucial and cannot be skipped as it's what assures our character measures up to our calling.

Wonderlust tip #9

The most glorious wins are often the unexpected ones. The delay might make you feel behind schedule but even 11:59 is before midnight.

Wonderlust tip #10

No one is going to give you a reward for how long you can stay in a relationship that you shouldn't be in (even if there are children involved). Choosing yourself and what's best for you isn't selfish, it's healthy.

Wonderlust tip #11

Identifying your love language is one of the healthiest things you can do for yourself and your relationship. It gives you permission to love and be loved in the way you need.

Wonderlust tip #12

Evaluate your mindset as it pertains to your current line of work and how you carry it out. If you're not completely satisfied, creating new thinking around old mindsets will help you shift towards more innovative approaches and enhance your productivity.

Wonderlust tip #13

Perspective is the key to all things. We might not be able to change our circumstances, but we have complete control over the power we give those circumstances to affect us.

Wonderlust tip #14

The more you understand fear, the less power it has over you.

Wonderlust tip #15

Pick up a business or financial literacy book and challenge yourself to make a financial move you have never done. No step is too small. I have included some resources in the *My Favorite Things* section in the back of the book.

Wonderlust tip #16

God meets us at the point of our effort. Do your part so that He can in turn do His. Start with what you have, and in due time the next steps will be revealed.

Wonderlust tip #17

Passion is transferable and so is apathy. Mind the company you keep.

Wonderlust tip #18

Categorize your community based on lead characters, supporting roles, and extras. Consider how much of your time and zeal you are investing in any of those people at any given point in time.

Wonderlust tip #19

We don't have to be convinced of wonder. Wonder makes a statement all on its own.

Wonderlust tip #20

Transferring Belief is the passing on of certainty which creates opportunities for real transformation beyond the inspiration of the moment.

Wonderlust tip #21

Borrowed Belief serves as a placeholder until you reach a place where you are able to establish your own.

WONDERLUST

About the Author

Rosie Ortiz is a keynote speaker, women's empowerment coach, and expert at helping women find their Wonder-Factor. She is the go-to source for helping others find solutions for a better more fulfilling life past learning challenges, stumbling blocks, and inner conflict. Rosie speaks for brands, companies, and groups of all sizes on her core message of inspiring women from all walks of life to be FREE, think boldly, lead bravely, and live a life of purpose!

When she's not on stage speaking, her next favorite thing to do is travel the world with her husband and kids. She enjoys afternoon tea, massages, and old musicals. Though she lives in Tampa she claims to be a Miami girl at heart.

WONDERLUST

BOOK ROSIE

To book Rosie Ortiz to speak at an upcoming event, please contact:

sky@wonderinyourwoman.com

CALL FOR STORIES

Do you have a story about how you found the Wonder in your Woman? We would love to hear it. Please send us your stories:

rosie@wonderinyourwoman.com

Visit

Wonderinyourwoman.com/wonderlust

For your "FREE BOOK BONUSES" to include:

Printable Wonderlust Affirmations

Printable Wonderlust Inventory

Printable Wonderlust Tips

www.ingramcontent.com/pod-product-compliance
Lightning Source LLC
LaVergne TN
LVHW041623070426
835507LV00008B/417